The Soul of
Prince Caspian

The Soul of
Prince Caspian

EXPLORING SPIRITUAL TRUTH
in the LAND *of* NARNIA

GENE VEITH

David C Cook®
transforming lives together

THE SOUL OF PRINCE CASPIAN
Published by David C. Cook
4050 Lee Vance View
Colorado Springs, CO 80918 U.S.A.

David C. Cook Distribution Canada
55 Woodslee Avenue, Paris, Ontario, Canada N3L 3E5

David C. Cook U.K., Kingsway Communications
Eastbourne, East Sussex BN23 6NT, England

David C. Cook and the graphic circle C logo
are registered trademarks of Cook Communications Ministries.

Scripture taken from *The Holy Bible, English Standard Version.*
Copyright © 2000; 2001 by Crossway Bibles, a division of Good News Publishers.
Used by permission. All rights reserved.

LCCN 2007939848
ISBN 978-0-7814-4528-3

© 2008 Gene Veith
Published in association with the literary agency of Jan P. Dennis,
19350 Glen Hollow Circle, Monument, CO 80132.

The Team: Gudmund Lee, Jaci Schneider, Karen Athen
Cover/Interior Design: Studiogearbox, Chris Gilbert

Cover Photo: Steve Gardner/Pixelworks Studio
©Jupiter Images

Printed in the United States of America
First Edition 2008

1 2 3 4 5 6 7 8 9 10

113007

To Samuel Clive Hensley

May you enjoy—and understand—the Narnia books as much as your mother did.

ACKNOWLEDGMENTS

Thanks to my colleagues and students at Patrick Henry College, who put up with me writing a book while also trying to master my new job.

I also want to acknowledge and to thank my wife, Jackquelyn, for enduring with me an unusually challenging year. We are stiff twin compasses.

And thanks to my editor, Gudmund Lee, for whipping my manuscript into shape.

CONTENTS

INTRODUCTION
A STORY WITHIN A STORY

C. S. Lewis is considered by many to be one of the greatest allegorical Christian writers of our time. And though his works include such masterpieces as *Mere Christianity, Till We Have Faces,* and *The Screwtape Letters,* the legacy of seven small children's stories—known as The Chronicles of Narnia—is what solidified his place in history. And now with the release of a series of Disney movies based off those books, we have new reason not only to celebrate these timeless tales, but also to explore their meanings.

The first book in the series, *The Lion, the Witch and the Wardrobe,* is arguably the best known of the seven. And rightfully so, for in that book readers discover the land of Narnia—a magical world of lampposts and fauns and talking animals—and, most importantly, of the Christ-figure Aslan, the king of beasts who would lay down his life for a sinful boy. Lewis enjoyed writing about the land of Narnia so much that, soon after he finished *The Lion, the Witch and the Wardrobe,* he dashed off a second book, which would become *Prince Caspian,* in less than a year, finishing it by the end of 1949. However, *The Lion, the Witch and the Wardrobe* had not made it entirely through the publishing process at that time and was not officially released until the fall of 1950, which meant that Lewis had finished *Prince Caspian* before he had any idea how his stories would be received.

Interestingly enough, when Lewis first began writing these books, no one saw them as we do now. In fact, the initial reception was rather underwhelming. Lewis biographer George Sayer described the lukewarm response of the critics:

> With few exceptions, the reviews of the Narnia books were cautious. Occasionally, they were hostile. At the time the books appeared, the real-life children's story was in fashion. It was commonly believed then that stories should help children to understand and relate to real life, that they should not encourage them to indulge in fantasies, and that fairy stories, if for any children at all, should only be for the very young. Some reviewers disliked the Narnia books for their Christian content, perhaps finding the parallels with the gospel story embarrassing, and further objected to the "indoctrination" of children. Of course, for many there was too much moralizing. Others attacked them because they contained "unnaturally unpleasant children" and too many violent and frightening incidents.[1]

And yet, reports Sayer, "despite all the reviewers' apprehensions, children loved the Narnia stories."[2] Their original publisher, Geoffrey Bles, doubted that the books would sell and worried that they would damage Lewis's reputation and hurt the sales of his other books.[3] But soon the publisher was calling for a whole series. Lewis wrote madly, and the publisher released a new Narnia book every year for the next six years. *Prince Caspian* was published in 1951.

RESTORING THE FAITH

In March 1961, ten years after *Prince Caspian*'s publication, Lewis wrote a letter to a girl named Anne; these books about Narnia were much more than just children's stories. In the letter, Lewis explained to Anne how "the whole Narnian story is about Christ." He told her how the lion Aslan is a symbol for Christ because, among other reasons, "Christ is called 'The Lion of Judah' in the Bible." Lewis then lays out his intentions for each book in the series. *Prince Caspian,* Lewis said, has to do with the "restoration of the true religion after corruption."[4]

Whereas *The Lion, the Witch and the Wardrobe* centers on the foundations of Christianity—the sacrificial death and resurrection of Jesus Christ for the salvation of all peoples—*Prince Caspian* contains some of Lewis's most searching criticisms of the "corruption" of our modern faith. It shows what happens when people forget everything that so captivated us in the first book—talking animals, the wonder and heroism of Narnia, and the power of the king.

And so, drawing on ideas that Lewis developed in his other works of apologetics and cultural criticism, *Prince Caspian* addresses the modern mind-set that has literally "forgotten" Christ and all He means to the world. In *Prince Caspian*'s Narnia, people no longer believe in lions, much less in Aslan. The world has dismissed its own past in favor of "progress" through the belief that whatever is new *must* be better than what is old. The people ridicule the old values of honor and integrity, they are convinced that the material world is all that matters, and they have sacrificed their personal freedom in favor of corrupt politicians and arbitrary rules.

Does any of this sound familiar to you? Yes, *Prince Caspian* is a fantastic story about the magical land of Narnia. But it is also a story about what is happening in *our* world. That is to say, *Prince Caspian* is about the same conflicts we find ourselves struggling with in today's post-Christian culture. The Christian consensus that formed our Western tradition has lost its authority. Secularism reigns. So what are we to do about it?

Lewis always insisted that Christianity is more than just a helpful belief system or some inner experience capable of offering some subjective meaning to life. For Lewis, Christianity is *true*, and he is concerned with restoring the faith. The objective, historical, absolute truth of Christianity means that believers can cling to Christ in faith despite what their subjective feelings might be telling them at any given time. But in a world that has been turned so far on its head, it is not enough just to come out and *say* that. One has to *show* it, but in a way that appeals to both the intellect *and* the imagination. Or as Lewis puts it, "Sometimes fairy stories may say best what's to be said."[5]

And so this book that you are holding will explore what *Prince*

Caspian has to say about the ideas and issues that Christians struggle with today. In doing so, this book will draw connections to other Lewis writings and show how he has used a children's story to say what otherwise might be considered a rather weighty topic. The ultimate goal, of course, is to help you, the reader, make the link between Narnia and your own life, so that the restoration of faith might take place in both worlds.

—Gene Veith

One

POINTS OF VIEW: DEFAMILIARIZING WHAT YOU KNOW

I wonder where we are and what it all means?
—Peter, upon the children's arrival in Narnia, chapter 2

Just as in *The Lion, the Witch and the Wardrobe, Prince Caspian* begins realistically enough. The four Pevensie children—Peter, Susan, Edmund, and Lucy—are waiting for a train. A year has passed since their adventure in the wardrobe. They are in a melancholy mood at the train station because the holidays are over and they are headed back to school. That is, they are headed back to that peculiarly British institution of the boarding school, in which very young children of well-to-do families live away from their parents for most of the year—an institution celebrated in *Harry Potter* but hated by the young C. S. Lewis, who had to endure the experience himself.

Suddenly, the children feel themselves pulled off the platform.

They hold on to each other, but something is yanking them into the air. The train station fades from their view, and the next thing they know they are in a dense forest. They do not quite realize it yet, but they are in Narnia, this time without the benefit of a wardrobe.

Lewis once said that various mental images provided the catalyst for his Narnia stories, and the one that got him started with *Prince Caspian* was that of a conjuring trick told from a different point of view.[1] In the standard magic act, a magician waves his wand, and, in a cloud of smoke, a person suddenly appears. Lewis wondered what this experience would have been like for the conjured person. He must have come from somewhere, right? So Lewis imagined someone going about his daily business, only to get pulled away suddenly in a cloud of smoke. This image is how Lewis came up with the idea of having the children, in the words of the original title, "drawn into Narnia."[2]

Similar uses of "point of view" take place throughout the novel. For instance, just as any child would do, Peter, Susan, Edmund, and Lucy soon begin exploring their new surroundings. They find a stream, apple trees, collapsed walls, and various ruins. Eventually it dawns on them that they have been exploring Cair Paravel, their old home in Narnia, only now it is in shambles, as if it had been neglected for a *very* long time. What they at first saw as undistinguished mounds and stones, they begin to see as familiar territory, charged with good memories. They had been looking at the same things all along, but a subtle shift in point of view allows them to really see.

Later in the story, the title character, Prince Caspian, bumps his head and is terrified to be awakened by a strange hairy face peering down on him. When it talks, this bestial apparition is even more unsettling. But what Caspian first experiences as a horrifying monster, he soon comes to know as a friendly talking badger. The creature is frightening to Caspian at first because he is unfamiliar with it, but these feelings quickly change once Caspian gains a better understanding of the situation. Again, this subtle shift in point of view helps one of Lewis's characters see things a little differently.

Perhaps the most important distinction Lewis makes in the novel is between the points of view of the "Old Narnians" versus the "New Narnians" (the Telmarines). Throughout the novel, Old Narnians and New Narnians see the same things—the woods, the sea, the lion—but come to completely different conclusions. Whether a character believes the lion is just another animal or the Lord of Narnia depends on his point of view. This is most evident in the differences between the young Prince Caspian and his evil uncle Miraz, king of the Telmarines. Miraz believes in a narrow, materialistic world that he can control. Caspian believes in a bigger world—one that includes both the seen and the unseen—even to the point that he tries to teach his pet dogs and cats to talk! Miraz doesn't believe in lions; Caspian believes in *the* lion.

Fiction, by its very nature, operates through point of view. When we read a story, we enter the mind of a fictional character— we see what he sees, feel what he feels, and vicariously share his experience. The imaginative experience of assuming different characters' points of view is part of what makes reading fiction so pleasurable, so the fact that Lewis's characters have different points of view in and of itself is not very profound. But Lewis is trying to do much more than simply differentiate between the points of view of his characters or show how they change throughout the novel—he is trying to illuminate our points of view as readers. He is using a fantastic story to help us as readers experience biblical truth—to see with new eyes what we might now take for granted.

POINT OF VIEW AND WORLDVIEW

In fiction that deals with ideas, such as the Narnia stories, points of view often embody and give us entry into different belief systems and ways of looking at the world. This is why reading imaginative fiction—not just The Chronicles of Narnia, but also other novels from a wide range of authors—can be so informative. It is one reason why, to quote Lewis again, "sometimes fairy stories may say best what's to be said."[3]

Christians today talk quite a bit about "worldview." In books, sermons, and classrooms, Christians have been exploring what the Bible teaches about reality and how biblical paradigms are in conflict with the views of life projected by other ideologies and religions.[4]

Worldviews are not, however, just sets of theoretical concepts or abstract ideas. They are, if you will excuse the literalism, ways of viewing the world. Two people can stand in the same forest and stare at the same wildlife. One will pick up on nature's intricate design and marvel at the order evident at every level of creation. The other will see a purely random chain of events. Two people can experience the same tragedy, like the death of a loved one. One will mourn at the sadness of our fallen, sin-wracked condition, but have hope in Christ's promise of everlasting life. The other will mourn at the absurdity of a life that has no meaning. In each case, the difference is not in the evidence or in the experience, but in the worldview each person brings to that evidence or experience.

Worldviews are the glasses through which people peer out at the world. Some people, as we say, look at the world through rose-colored glasses. Others keep their shades on all the time and never see the light. With that idea in mind, John Calvin compared the Bible to a different set of glasses, one through which we can see the world more clearly:

> For by the Scripture as our guide and teacher, [the Lord] not only makes those things plain which would otherwise escape our notice, but almost compels us to behold them; as if he had assisted our dull sight with spectacles.[5]

Clearly, religious beliefs shape a person's worldview, but so does culture. Even people who do not think much about such big issues operate within a specific worldview, which they have simply absorbed through their social surroundings. Worldviews are not just taught; we might say, they are caught. Family, friends, the entertainment industry, and the social set we want to belong to all shape our innermost assumptions. Some professed Christians operate with a worldview shaped by their culture rather than by the Bible. If their peers accept extramarital sex and abortion, then they will as well. Christians who take their faith more seriously struggle with the disconnect between what they know of Scripture and what they see in the world today. They probably feel like Caspian trying in vain to teach his dogs and cats how to talk.

Furthermore, worldviews are very resistant. Counterarguments, facts, and even experiences are not enough to dislodge them. A person's worldview is the world his mind inhabits, an explanatory paradigm that accounts for everything he takes in. A materialistic atheist who believes that human beings are only animals and that existence is purely random can explain everything he sees in terms of his worldview. So can a New Age mystic, for whom the universe is an illusion and who believes that he is a god. So can a Christian, who believes that the universe is God's creation and that we are all sinful at heart and in need of God's redemption.

Some theologians, such as Abraham Kuyper and Cornelius Van Til, believe that everyone is imprisoned, so to speak, in his or her presuppositions—that is, his or her worldview. To have a Christian worldview requires an act of God's grace. Apologists who try to use rational arguments and evidence to prove the case of Christianity are fighting a losing battle. According to this view, since people's minds are self-contained, blocking out God's truth and inhabiting their own fallen ideologies, persuading them through rational means is impossible.

Ironically, these conservative Christians agree with today's secular postmodernists who believe that everyone is trapped in his or her own prison of mental and cultural constructions. Postmodernists believe that we can therefore never access any objective truth, since we cannot escape our own subjective frameworks and perspectives. Because everyone has his or her own worldview, and we have no way of proving that any of them is more valid than any other, truth is relative. Christian presuppositionalists are not relativists, though, and believe that the Bible offers the one true worldview. In fact, they deserve credit for anticipating decades ago what postmodernists are just now articulating.

Francis Schaeffer agreed with Van Til and the presuppositional apologists, but he, like some of them, argued that non-Christian worldviews are so incomplete that no one can consistently live by them. Our materialistic atheist friend, for instance, probably regards his children as more than animals and loves them with a transcendent commitment that completely contradicts his worldview, which cannot account for transcendent values. Schaeffer's approach to evangelism was to uncover the internal contradictions of an unbeliever's worldview, "taking the roof off," so to speak, as a way to open him to God's Word.[6]

C. S. Lewis, as an apologist, was not a presuppositionalist. In *Mere Christianity*, for example, he uses rational argument to make the case for Christianity, which he believes is objectively true and more or less accessible to a reasonable mind despite one's worldview. And yet, Lewis was well aware of the different worldviews people inhabit. In his scholarly book *The Discarded Image*, Lewis explores the Ptolomaic model of the universe—the view that the earth is the center around which the planets and the stars rotate—as the backdrop for Greek, Roman, medieval, and Renaissance literature.

But in his imaginative works, such as The Chronicles of Narnia, Lewis attempts another kind of Christian apologetics. He does something similar to Francis Schaeffer—he exploits the imagination in an attempt to simultaneously expose false worldviews and show how the Christian worldview is so much bigger, more wonderful, and true. This is especially evident in *Prince Caspian*.

Which brings us back to my earlier point that Lewis is not trying simply to differentiate between different points of view, but rather to use the convention of "story" to illuminate our points of view as readers, to give us a new appreciation for the Christian faith and the worldview it makes possible. But how exactly does he do this? And to what end? He does this through a literary technique known as "defamiliarizing."

Defamiliarization

Many people, non-Christian and Christian alike, have come to see biblical doctrine as boring at best and oppressively burdensome at worst. Lewis explodes these misconceptions, showing how wonderful, liberating, and deeply satisfying the Christian worldview is by defamiliarizing biblical truth. That is, he takes something so familiar as to be taken for granted and presents it from an unusual angle, causing the reader to see it in a new light and experience it as if for the first time.

The opening of *Prince Caspian*, when the children arrive in a strange new world only to discover that it is their old home, is reminiscent of a story G. K. Chesterton once told: "I have often had a fancy for writing a romance about an English yachtsman who slightly miscalculated his course and discovered England under the impression that it was a new island in the South Seas." Chesterton imagines a "man who landed (armed to the teeth and talking by signs) to plant the British flag on that barbaric temple which turned out to be the Pavilion at Brighton." Though such an ironic scenario is comical, Chesterton draws from it a serious point: "What could be more delightful than to have in the same few minutes all the fascinating terrors of going abroad combined with all the humane security of coming home again?"[7]

Chesterton, who was one of Lewis's favorite writers and whose books were instrumental in his coming to Christianity, then relates the hypothetical tale to his own life and to his faith:

> I have a peculiar reason for mentioning the man in a yacht, who discovered England. For I am that man in a yacht. I discovered England.... When I fancied that I stood alone I was really in the ridiculous position of being backed up by all Christendom. It may be, Heaven forgive me, that I did try to be original; but I only succeeded in inventing all by myself an inferior copy of the existing traditions of civilized religion. The man from the yacht thought he was the first to find England; I thought I was the first to find Europe. I did try to found a heresy of my own; and when I had put the last touches to it, I discovered that it was orthodoxy.[8]

Chesterton had scorned the Christianity of his childhood, but in his search for truth, he discovered an amazing new world, which turned out to be the Christianity of his childhood! The man in the story was looking at his homeland from a new angle. He did not see it as he used to. It was no longer ordinary, but seen from this fresh perspective, it was exciting and exotic. Chesterton was making a joke about the Brighton Pavilion, a grandiose Taj Mahal–like palace and a British tourist trap. But while the British are so famil-iar with it that they consider it old hat, I suspect that we Americans *would* find the Brighton Pavilion exciting and exotic.

This is a clue to how *all* literature works—indeed, how all art forms work—and how literature and art can enrich our lives. Most of us know the old saying that "familiarity breeds con-tempt." The Russian literary critic Victor Shklovsky takes this one step further, showing how familiarity decreases perception; that is, familiarity makes us stop noticing things, makes us liter-ally see less. A work of art, though, whether a painting or a novel, can take a subject so familiar that we have stopped paying atten-tion to it and cause us to contemplate it again. "Art," Shklovsky said, "increases our perception, our ability to see something, whereas habitualization devours work, clothes, furniture, one's wife, and the fear of war."9

A job may start out stimulating, enjoyable, and fulfilling. But once it becomes a habit, the worker goes on autopilot and the joy disappears. A woman may buy a new dress but will soon grow tired of it. A new sofa at first dominates the room but then fades into the background. More tragically, marriages go bad when spouses take each other for granted. Even horrible experiences—like the fear of war—can become mundane. "And so," Shklovsky said, "life is reck-oned as nothing."10

The same deadening effect of habit can happen to a person's faith. The thrill of belief can fade. Christianity can come to seem ho-hum. Going to church week after week can become routine. The Bible can lose its edge. Many once-zealous Christians begin to think sermons and worship and theology are boring.

Boredom has been called the characteristic spiritual problem of our age. In our current media environment, we are hyperstimulated. With our TVs constantly on at home, our iPods blaring when we get in our cars, and our computers deluging us with information at work, our minds are constantly bombarded. That bombardment is designed to give us pleasure, to keep us entertained. But ironically, it increases boredom. Just as drug addicts have to keep taking bigger doses to get high, we must have more and more stimulation to keep us interested. (This is also why our popular entertainment has to keep getting more extreme—more shocking, more gruesome, more pornographic—to break through our growing insensibility.) And when the bombardment slows— when we have to endure silence, when we have to do something that is not fun but necessary, when we have to attend to someone other than ourselves—we can hardly handle that at all.

But it isn't necessarily the fault of a person's job that he no longer sees the significance of his employment as a divine calling and a means of loving and serving God and one's neighbor.[11] It isn't the fault of a set of clothes or a piece of furniture that the owner gets tired of it. And it is seldom the fault of the wife when her husband no longer appreciates her. If we become calloused toward war, or to other people's suffering, or to our blessings, or to love, this is just more evidence for what the Bible calls our hardness of heart.

Nor is it the fault of the church that our hearts are dulled to the point that we are oblivious to the presence of Christ. (Many churches, ironically, try to play the same game of hyperstimulation with action-packed services and numerous activities, oblivious to how they are contributing to the problem.) "There is no such thing as an uninteresting subject," observed Chesterton. "The only thing that can exist is an uninterested person."[12]

This dull insensitivity to life and to God is a moral and spiritual problem. The old Christian theologians identified it as a species of the sin "sloth," a form of laziness. A person who expects the universe to keep him entertained and is indignant when it doesn't is lazy. But his is also a failure of imagination.

Shklovsky believed that art, by presenting its subject from an unusual point of view, defamiliarizes the routine. The formal structures of art and the different contexts it creates increase our perception. Most people never take a second look at the bowl of fruit in their kitchen, but take that bowl of fruit out of the kitchen, put it into a painting, and hang it on a museum wall—as in a Dutch Master still life—and people will marvel at its beauty. They will appreciate the texture of the orange peel, the bruises on the apple, and the light reflecting off the bowl. Ironically, the beauty in the painting is *the same beauty* as in the kitchen. But we never notice the fruit in the kitchen, because it is so familiar. The painting, though, causes us to pay attention to these forms and colors, appreciating their aesthetic impact. If we are wise, we will carry the lesson from the museum back into our ordinary lives, so that we might pay attention and appreciate what we have in the "kitchen," whatever that might be.

For instance, a man might, through many years of familiarity, take his wife for granted. But if he reads a novel about love and marriage, and the novel's point of view causes him to identify with the characters, he might see his own marriage reflected in the plot of the novel. As he reads and contemplates this imaginary relationship, he might learn to notice and appreciate his own wife once again.

SO WHAT'S THE CATCH?

Art and literature *can* enrich our daily routines, and they *can* help us become more sensitive to the subtle beauties of our own lives by defamiliarizing what we might otherwise overlook. But art and literature do not *always* have this effect. Some people today take this too far and find meaning *only* by losing themselves in books or other "art forms" such as TV and movies and video games. A disturbing trend has grown in the world of virtual gaming in which people are now able to create online alternate realities where they can live out their lives as completely different people. In theory this might sound like fun, but in actuality things like this only serve to *increase* dissatisfaction and magnify boredom. Similarly, the married man above could read a novel that promotes an escapist sexual fantasy in his mind, motivating him to divorce his real wife in search of an idealized storybook woman who does not exist. The path toward a greater appreciation for the things in your life does not include forgetting them entirely.

Shklovsky said that the way art defamiliarizes is by its aesthetic form, which makes perception more difficult. It takes work of the imagination to decipher, interpret, and contemplate a good novel, drama, or painting. Some works of art, however, have little aesthetic form. They are immediately accessible, make no demands, and do not cause the reader to think. These works of poor aesthetic quality seldom defamiliarize their subjects. Instead of possessing their own aesthetic forms, they tend to be conventional, following the same plots and employing the same character types as every other example of their genre. They are, in short, *familiar*, works of mere entertainment that end up contributing to boredom.

Soap operas and romance novels might, through their fantasies, tempt a spouse to commit adultery. But a great novel like Tolstoy's *Anna Karenina*, though about adultery, never would, because *Anna Karenina* is precisely *about* the foolishness of a woman who succumbs to these romantic escapist fantasies and who learns how futile they are as they destroy her life. What makes good art "good," among other things, is its honesty, its fidelity to truth presented in all its complexity. A bad use of the imagination can indeed lead us astray, but the good use of the imagination can help us stay on the right path.

Thus our aesthetic taste has a moral dimension. This does not have as much to do with the content (whether or not a work contains violence or sexuality) as it does with how that content is presented—that is, its form. Works of art that are true and good and beautiful can defamiliarize our lives. This entails not just staying in the imaginary realm, but bringing back its lessons to illuminate the real world, as Lewis did in The Chronicles of Narnia.

BRINGING THE MESSAGE BACK TO LIFE

C. S. Lewis began his series of children's stories in an attempt to defamiliarize Christianity and wrote *Prince Caspian* in particular in an attempt to defamiliarize the loss of faith. As we discussed elsewhere,[13] Lewis, who became a Christian as an adult, marveled at the way the astonishing, breathtaking truths of Christianity—that

God became Man, that He bore the sins of the world and paid their penalty, that limitless joy awaits us after death—have somehow, to believers and nonbelievers alike, become humdrum and mundane.

He remembered being taken to church as a child and leaving with little impression made. Lewis blamed this on the fact that adults would tell him how he was supposed to feel about Jesus and the artificial reverence with which he was supposed to approach Bible stories. But surely the problem was not with Christianity itself, but with what Victor Shklovsky described earlier: For young Jack Lewis, the Christianity of his childhood—apparently presented in an inept way—was just another habit. It became so familiar that he never thought about it. And when he wanted to escape his overly familiar, mundane life, such as when he went off to school and university, Christianity was one of the many dull things he left behind.

This is probably true not just for a young C. S. Lewis, but for many of us who were raised in the church. Christianity's familiarity has helped it fade from our personal and cultural consciousness. The ramifications of our beliefs are still present in our moral assumptions, our laws, and our institutions, but few people notice them anymore. Thankfully Lewis decided not just to give us another set of reasons to believe Christian dogma, but rather he chose to show us how faith in Christ can be exhilarating. He presents Christianity from a fresh point of view, causing us to notice the wonder of what it has always been.

Sometimes his use of logical reasoning *is* one of these fresh approaches, since our culture has long forgotten the intellectual dimension of Christianity. But he also uses imaginative and artistic devices to open our eyes to what the old-time religion is actually saying. Consider this famous passage from *Mere Christianity:*

> I am trying here to prevent anyone saying the really foolish thing that people often say about Him: "I'm ready to accept Jesus as a great moral teacher, but I don't accept His claim to be God." That is one thing we must not say. A man who was merely a man and said the sort of thing Jesus said would not be a great moral teacher. He would either be a lunatic—on a level with the man who says he is a poached egg—or else he would be the Devil of Hell. You must make your choice. Either this man was, and is, the Son of God: or else a madman or something worse. You can shut Him up for a fool, you can spit at Him and kill Him as a demon or you can fall at His feet and call Him Lord and God. But let us not come with any patronizing nonsense about His being a great human teacher. He has not left that open to us. He did not intend to.[14]

The argument itself is an old one, a classic defense of the deity of Christ. But Lewis breathes life into his logic with lively language and vivid imagery, going so far as to throw in a poached egg. To most of us raised in a culture in which even believers treat Christianity as something nonrational, this is *unfamiliar*. And that is precisely the point. Defamiliarizing Christianity *was* Lewis's explicit intention for *Prince Caspian* and The Chronicles of Narnia. By his own admission, Lewis intends to reopen our eyes, to help us see as we have never seen before—or at least as we haven't seen in a very long time: "Supposing that by casting all these things into an imaginary world, stripping them of their stained-glass and Sunday school associations, one could make them for the first time appear in their potency?"[15] Fitting, then, that these are children's stories, since it's apparent that Lewis would have us see as children do: with awe and wonder. And though *Prince Caspian* reveals the unhappy truth of what can happen to individuals and cultures that lose their faith, more importantly, it reminds us of the joy and excitement that the restoration of those beliefs can bring back into our lives.

STUDY QUESTIONS

1. A "worldview" has to do with the set of assumptions people have about reality. What are some elements of a Christian worldview? From the perspective of a Christian worldview, what are human beings like, and why should they be valued?

2. What are some things you see contributing to your worldview specifically? Make a list. This could include circumstances, experiences, influences, beliefs, and so on.

3. In what ways do you think your point of view affects your perception of reality and consequently your actions? What do you think would happen if you intentionally tried to picture certain events from an alternate point of view? What about you would change?

4. Have you ever had a sense of recognition while experiencing a work of art—a book, a photograph, a film, a painting—in which something you had taken for granted was "defamiliarized," causing you to notice it in a new way? When? Take some time to see the movie *Prince Caspian* when it releases in spring 2008, either by yourself or with friends and family. Note for yourself the ways in which your faith is defamiliarized through the movie.

5. What are some things in your own life that risk becoming so familiar that you stop appreciating them? What changes could you make in your everyday life to avoid that?

6. Like Lewis, in what ways has your faith become a habit? What might a daily faith experience full of awe and wonder look like to you? What examples of that kind of faith can you find in the Bible? What steps can you take to experience that kind of faith once again?

Two
PROGRESS: TELMARINES AND MODERNISTS

He remembered that he was, after all, a Telmarine,
one of the race who cut down trees wherever they
could and were at war with all wild things.

—chapter 5

As mentioned earlier, perhaps the greatest conflict in *Prince Caspian* is that between the "Old Narnians" (the talking animals, dwarfs, and other throwbacks to the ancient world) and who we might call by extension the "New Narnians" (the ruling Telmarines who seek to stamp out anything that does not recognize and represent their "new" way of life and anything that might impede their "progress").

In his other writings, C. S. Lewis also deals with the conflict between the ancient world and the modern world—the worldviews of the past and the worldviews of the present. He often challenges our modern trust in progress, the assumption that things are getting better and better and will continue to do so until all our problems are solved. Unfortunately, belief in progress necessarily assumes that the past is something we must put behind us, that the traditional must be rejected as "old-fashioned" or "out of date." Instead, Lewis highlights what our modern culture has lost in jettisoning its foundation, and he shows how the insights of the past—particularly, historic Christianity—can speak precisely to our contemporary condition.

In *Prince Caspian*, the Telmarines are the "modernists" of Narnia. They reject the supernatural and despoil the natural; they twist education so that it ignores the past and diminishes human experience. They rule everything absolutely. The Telmarines and their rule thus constitute the exact parallel for what Christians must contend against in our world.

MODERN NARNIA

So, exactly how much time elapsed in Narnia between the Pevensie children's first visit and this one? Clearly something has changed since their experience with the wardrobe. Their beloved castle, Cair Paravel, is overgrown by forest, and the landscape is significantly altered—things that could not just happen overnight. Lewis would later create a time line of Narnian history, according to which the gap between *The Lion, the Witch and the Wardrobe* and *Prince Caspian* is precisely 1,288 years.[1]

One thousand two hundred eighty-eight years is a long time. Here in our world, that would put us back in the Dark Ages, between the fall of Rome and the rise of medieval civilization. We have certainly progressed a great deal since then, as our technology can attest. Airplanes, electricity, computers, and health care all give us huge advantages over our eighth-century ancestors. They huddled around their fires and hoped not to die of the plague; we order takeout and turn up the volume on our plasma screens. Though some might not call this "progress," it is foolish to deny the reality of our technological advances, which have made possible certain comforts and luxuries that would have staggered the kings of old.

I believe we have made some moral and political progress as well. We no longer countenance slavery, for example, and much of the world now consists of democratic nations. True, the ancient Greeks invented democracy and the Romans created representative republics, while the tyrannies of fascism and communism are modern inventions. But on the whole, today we are surely freer, more equal, and more self-governing than our ancestors were in the past. Though whether we have their fortitude, courage, and character may be a different story.

Yet isn't it curious that, in Narnia, not much has changed besides the landscape after twelve centuries? King Miraz lives in a castle, just like Peter, Susan, Edmund, and Lucy did. The Telmarines wear armor and fight with swords, just as in Old Narnia. In fact, the Telmarines still dress the same, eat the same foods, and follow the same political system as their counterparts did over a thousand years earlier. Apparently the Telmarines were not all that great when it came to science and engineering, either. More than a thousand years after King Peter ruled at Cair Paravel, Narnia is still stuck in the Middle Ages.

What *has* changed, of course, is their worldview. The values, the beliefs, and the religion of what we might call the modern

Narnia are very different from those of the old days. And though the material culture seems to be the same, we are told that New Narnia is "an unhappy country."[2] Miraz is a tyrant, collecting high taxes, enforcing harsh laws, and exercising cruelty. Narnia, following the worldview of the Telmarines, has become a narrow, restrictive place, void of wonder, mystery, and freedom.

It is clear, however, that science and technology progress because knowledge in those fields builds and accumulates. In the distant past, someone invented the wheel. Because it did not need to be reinvented, other people throughout the generations added systems of suspension and propulsion and, more recently, gasoline engines and automatic transmissions. By ourselves, few if any of us could build an automobile from scratch any better than our eighth-century ancestors could, but thankfully we do not have to. We can drive because we stand on the shoulders of numerous generations of inventors. And with new fuel sources and greater safety devices, that automobile will continue to be improved upon beyond what we can see today.

All this progress in technology creates the illusion that we are also making progress in every other sphere of life. While it is true that the newest computer is likely to be superior to yesterday's model, it does not follow that the newest *theologies* are superior to older ones. And the irony is that, while our technological progress builds upon past discoveries, in our theology, morality, and other areas of life—including philosophy, art, and family values—we keep starting over, as if generations of human experience mean nothing. We refuse to let those kinds of wisdom accumulate. We keep reinventing the wheel.

But by casting Old and New Narnia in virtually the same light, save for a few minor geographical changes, Lewis ingeniously takes technological progress off the table. We are left to judge only the allegedly progressive ideals and mind-set of modern Narnian culture. And in these issues, the Telmarines are in basic agreement with our modern-day secularists.

MODERN THOUGHT

The word "modern" suggests "right now, in the present time." But in reality the habit of mind and the worldview that define "modernity" began some three centuries ago. In fact, many people now consider "modern" to be old-fashioned. Now we are "postmodern." But postmodernism itself is, arguably, a phase of the modern impulse. And it was a distinct brand of "modernism" that Lewis battled, both in his works of Christian apologetics and in his fiction, particularly *Prince Caspian*.

Modernity—that is, the condition of being modern—began in the 1700s in the paradigm shift known as the Enlightenment. The very term implies that everything prior to this time period was in darkness. Of course, the light that the word "Enlightenment" refers to was "reason," so that this period is also called the Age of Reason. But not so much in the sense of logic and abstract thinking—the ancient and medieval ages certainly had that—but rather scientific reason, thought grounded in empirical research and common sense. Above all, the Enlightenment considered its brand of thinking to be free—free from the restrictions of tradition, superstition, and religion.

And science indeed made great strides in the eighteenth century.

People, using their intellects alone, made discovery after discovery, giving rational explanations for what before had been utter mysteries. This new science was revealing the underlying laws of nature itself. Sir Isaac Newton reduced to mathematical regularity the laws of gravity, the movement of the planets, the properties of light, and the laws of motion. The impact Newton had on the world is well expressed by a great poet of the time, Alexander Pope:

> Nature and nature's laws lay hid in night;
> God said "Let Newton be" and all was light.[3]

Newton himself was a strong Bible believer (though reportedly weak on the doctrine of the Trinity), but notice the religious shift. Laws were now of "nature," not God, and revelation was now from a scientist, not God's Word. Denizens of the eighteenth century did believe in God. They believed that the rationality they were discovering in nature was evidence of a rational mind that created it all. A watch, they would argue, is evidence for a watchmaker. And nature is an even more intricate machine than a watch. Thus, anticipating "intelligent design" theory, Enlightenment thinkers proved the existence of God.

But they rejected Christianity as a kind of "superstition." Any such mode of thought simply had to be rejected in the name of reason. Christianity is all about the supernatural. It evades scientific, empirical evidence. Reasonable people focus instead on what is natural. We cannot have miracles, the Enlightenment thinkers said, since the Divine Watchmaker would never interfere in the perfect natural order He Himself established. But if you take the miracles out of Christianity, not much remains.

Furthermore, Christianity is a *revealed* religion. The Enlightenment sought a religion based on reason and reason alone, but Christianity has too many doctrines that the human mind just cannot get itself around. The Trinity? Unreasonable! God becoming a Man? Unreasonable! One Man taking upon Himself the sins of the world? Unreasonable!

In the times of darkness people used to think that God caused it to rain. But that was just because they had no better answer. Thanks to empirical research, we now know that rain is caused by complex natural factors having to do with humidity, air pressure, and temperature. We don't need God anymore, the Enlightened ones thought, to account for why it rains. We perhaps need the *concept* of God to account for why the universe functions in such an orderly way that we can account for the weather, but that is as far as it goes.

In this new rational religion known as deism, the Divine Watchmaker sets the universe into motion, but then just watches it run. He does not interfere. Human beings are left basically on their own. In practice, deism resulted in a version of Christianity stripped bare of the supernatural. All that was left was morality. People were expected to live according to the utilitarian ethics of the day, doing what was useful for the rational machine of society to function smoothly. (Interestingly, deists believed in a heaven and hell, a realm where the good are rewarded and the evil are punished. They reasoned that, in this life, good people are often *not* rewarded while evil people often do very well for themselves, but such injustice is unreasonable! There must be a realm in which the Divine Watchmaker will balance the accounts.)

But though the deists needed God to account for the origins of creation, in the nineteenth century that need, too, would disappear. Evolution said, "Let Darwin be," and all was enlightened even more. Darwin was able to account for the origin of species, and of humanity itself, in the strict terms of a closed natural system. By extension, people began to assume that the universe itself was self-contained and uncreated. Furthermore, they assumed that the physical universe was all there is.

Notice that the theory of evolution itself is nothing more than the Enlightenment worldview of "progress" applied to biology— the notion that life itself emerged out of the primordial darkness and just keeps getting better and better. "Progress," the idea that what is old should be jettisoned in favor of the new, soon took over not just in intellectual fields but in society. During the Age of Reason, the French Revolution swept away the old medieval social order. Revolutionaries beheaded the royal family and vandalized churches. At the revolution's height, its supporters crowned a woman costumed to symbolize the Goddess of Reason in Notre Dame Cathedral. Reason, quite literally, took the place of God. True, the French Revolution degenerated into a Reign of Terror, and the dictatorship of Napoleon launched a world war, but that was the price of progress.

In the nineteenth century, trust in progress accelerated. Industrialism created vast amounts of new wealth. True, working conditions in the new factories were appalling, what with child labor and starvation wages. And, yes, the factories blackened the environment. And though crime, poverty, and war dominated the nineteenth century, such was the faith in progress that many were convinced the twentieth century would be the dreamed-of utopia in which all of these social problems—with the application of rational, scientific principles—would simply go away.

And the twentieth century was so convinced of progress that it turned "modernism" into an ideology. If something was "old-fashioned," whether a clothing style or a religious belief, it needed to be discarded. Modern art rejected the whole tradition of representational painting in favor of abstract designs. Modern literature sought brand-new ways of writing poetry and telling stories. Modern architecture stripped away all of that traditional ornamentation in favor of technologically impressive boxes of glass and steel. Modern theology subjected the Bible to a pseudoscientific analysis, which amounted to nothing more than rejecting its supernatural content, and tried to construct a new Christianity to sanctify social progress. The "new morality" replaced what was derided as "old" and "tired," supporting indulgences such as sex outside of marriage, which used to be called immoral.

True, the twentieth century saw some setbacks to progress as well. Those new ideologies that were supposed to usher in a social golden age—such as communism and fascism—ended up killing a lot of people. And the twentieth century, far from eliminating war and human misery, seemed to feature more of both than any other point in human history. But that was the price of progress.

LEWIS THE DINOSAUR

The notion that whatever is new is better than whatever is old is at the essence of the modern mind. Lewis referred to this as "the universal evolutionism of modern thought":

> By universal evolutionism I mean the belief that the very formula of universal process is from imperfect to perfect, from small beginnings to great endings, from the rudimentary to the elaborate: the belief which makes people find it natural to think that morality springs from savage taboos, adult sentiment from infantile sexual maladjustments, thought from instinct, mind from matter, organic from inorganic, cosmos from chaos. This is perhaps the deepest habit of mind in the contemporary world.[4]

This habit of mind is exactly what C. S. Lewis addressed as a Christian apologist, making the case for historical, supernatural Christianity to this "modern world." When Lewis became a professor at Cambridge in 1954, his inaugural lecture was entitled *De Descriptione Temporum*, that is, "Of Descriptions of the Times." In it he explores the "chasm" that separates the modern world from *everything* that had gone on before, which he believes "is the greatest change in the history of Western Man." He calls that earlier world, which encompasses everything from the ancient Greeks through Jane Austen, who died in 1817, "Old European" or "Old Western." Notice how this is reminiscent of "Old Narnia" in

Prince Caspian, which he had written six years earlier. Lewis concludes his lecture by calling himself a "dinosaur," a creature of the old world that his Cambridge students could at least study as a specimen.[5]

But if Lewis was a dinosaur let loose in the modern world, he was more like the tyrannosaur in *Jurassic Park* than a mere fossil. He simply proved more than a match for his modern-day counterparts.

For example, Lewis, using the tools of old-fashioned literary scholarship, demonstrated that, far from being based on objective science, the new materialistic shift in worldview came long before any alleged scientific discoveries. In his book *The Discarded Image*, a scholarly explanation of the Ptolomaic model of the universe, Lewis showed that theories of evolution actually preceded Darwin:

> When I was a boy I believed that "Darwin discovered evolution" and that the far more general, radical, and even cosmic developmentalism which till lately dominated all popular thought was a superstructure raised on the biological theorem.[6]

Lewis then cites statements from Schelling, Keats, Wagner, Goethe, Herder—in works dating from the early nineteenth century, well before Darwin published *The Origin of Species* in 1859—about cosmic progress and how life develops from the lower to the higher. And before that, such ideas appeared in eighteenth-century Enlightenment-era thinkers like Leibniz,

Akenside, Kant, Maupertuis, and Diderot. Lewis might have thrown in some commentary on what is surely the greatest poem on evolution and its spiritual implications: Tennyson's "In Memoriam A. H. H.," which was completed nine years *before* Darwin's book. Lewis concludes:

> The demand for a developing world—a demand obviously in harmony both with the revolutionary and the romantic temper—grows up first; when it is full grown the scientists go to work and discover the evidence on which our belief in that sort of universe would now be held to rest. There is no question here of the old Model's being shattered by the inrush of new phenomena. The truth would seem to be the reverse; that when changes in the human mind produce a sufficient disrelish of the old Model and a sufficient hankering for some new one, phenomena to support that new one will obediently turn up.[7]

Perhaps ironically, Lewis's critiques of modernity call to mind what the postmodernists are now saying about the Age of Reason, that rationalistic systems and scientists themselves construct "explanatory paradigms" that are culturally conditioned. The difference is that Lewis still believes in Truth.

Lewis consistently shows that for a period that began with the Age of Reason, modernity is not all that reasonable. Lewis identifies the logical fallacy of what he calls "chronological snobbery," which he defines as "the uncritical acceptance of the intellectual climate common to our own age and the assumption that whatever has gone out of date is on that account discredited." He says:

> You must find why it went out of date. Was it ever refuted (and if so by whom, where, and how conclusively) or did it merely die away as fashions do? If the latter, this tells us nothing about its truth or falsehood. From seeing this, one passes to the realization that our own age is also "a period," and certainly has, like all periods, its own characteristic illusions. They are likeliest to lurk in those widespread assumptions which are so ingrained in the age that no one dares to attack or feels it necessary to defend them.[8]

Lewis learned about chronological snobbery, as he describes in his autobiography, *Surprised by Joy*, from his friend Owen Barfield. It is the same point made by Lewis's literary mentor G. K. Chesterton:

> An imbecile habit has arisen in modern controversy of saying that such and such a creed can be held in one age but cannot be held in another. Some dogma, we are told, were credible in the 12th century, but are not credible in the 20th. You might as well say that a certain philosophy can be believed on Mondays, but cannot be believed on

Tuesdays. You might as well say of a view of the cosmos that it was suitable to half-past three, but not suitable for half-past four. What a man believes depends upon his philosophy, not upon the clock or the century.[9]

Lewis's critique of modernity was not aimed just at its scientific mode of thinking. Lewis believed the materialistic universe posited by modernist thought to be, despite its infinite expanse, a small, constricting, claustrophobic place. The pretensions of "scientism" squeeze out the very possibility of freedom and joy.

Furthermore, Lewis disliked the way modernity, in the name of progress, presumes to dominate, dissect, and even destroy the things of nature. He opposed the vivisection of animals—the practice of cruel treatment of animals in the name of scientific research—not because he was an animal-rights activist or a postmodernist convinced that there is no difference between human beings and animals, but rather because "once the old Christian idea of a total difference in kind between man and beast has been abandoned, then no argument for experiments on animals can be found which is not also an argument for experiments on inferior men."[10] His principle was not postmodern, but premodern: "The victory of vivisection marks a great advance in the triumph of ruthless, non-moral utilitarianism over the old world of ethical law."[11]

And like his friend J. R. R. Tolkien, he disliked modern developers' habit of cutting down too many trees. Tolkien's picture of Saruman's massive industrial complex built at the expense of Fangorn Forest is parallel to Lewis's complaints in *Prince Caspian* about the Telmarines, a race who "cut down trees whenever they could and were at war with all wild things."[12] This does not make Lewis a postmodern environmentalist, but rather a premodern conservationist. Lewis even wrote a poem on the subject titled "The Future of Forestry," which included the lines:

> How will the legend of the age of trees
> Feel, when the last tree falls in England?[13]

In *Prince Caspian*, the rebellion of the Old Narnians against the tree-chopping, lion-denying, progressive Telmarines represents the same war Lewis himself was conducting against modernism. Not that Lewis is suggesting that we disregard all of the positive benefits of modern thought. He is simply suggesting that we do not have to accept the current trends of our world without questioning the modern paradigms in which they come. We must instead open our eyes and our minds, just as Prince Caspian did, to recognize that there are deeper things in the world than what progressive modernists dream of.

STUDY QUESTIONS

1. In what ways do you sense that modern theologies have become "narrow, restrictive place[s], void of wonder, mystery, and freedom"? Do you see any of that in the Christian church? How have you experienced this personally?

2. How is the modernists' description of God as a Divine Watchmaker different from God's depiction in the Bible? Which of those descriptions do you adhere to in your daily life? (Be honest!) What can you do to ensure you are not settling for the notion of a Divine Watchmaker?

3. How has modern thought—which includes scientific reason, empirical evidence, and common sense—affected the church? Your own walk? How do you think God intends us to think of and experience Him?

4. Lewis suggests that we do not have to accept the current trends of our world without questioning the modern paradigms in which they come. What are some of the paradigms or trends you would like to question? Pray to God for wisdom and guidance in your thinking on those matters, and then look to His Word for some insight.

Three
REGRESS: OLD NARNIA

"I wish—I wish—I wish I could have lived in the Old Days."
—Prince Caspian to his uncle, chapter 4

As we saw in chapter 2, *Prince Caspian* frames its themes in terms of a conflict between old and new, or more precisely the "Old Narnians" and the "New Narnians." Lewis himself said that the book is about the restoration of what has been lost, and in his own scholarship he tends to champion old ideas against the pretensions of a new age.

Does this preference for the old over the new mean then that Christians should lean conservative not just in theology but on every issue? That is what some so-called culture warriors would have us believe. Indeed, there are many reasons why theologically conservative Christians tend to be conservative on other issues as well. But simply advocating a tradition because it is old seems just as invalid as advocating something because it is new; it is just another brand of "chronological snobbery." Surely a Christian's cultural agenda must go beyond trying to restore the past.

Lewis was aware of this as he wrote *Prince Caspian* and perhaps even more so in his other writings. Clearly he is making a case for "regress" instead of "progress," but what he is looking for in the past are not antiques or reactionary poses, but rather universal and timeless truths, which are suited to every age and culture—even our own.

THE GOLDEN AGE

At one point during the story Dr. Cornelius describes the reign of Peter, Susan, Edmund, and Lucy to Prince Caspian as Narnia's "Golden Age."[1] Ironically, while people today tend to believe in progress—the notion that everything gets better with time as we advance toward an ever-improving future—throughout history most people have believed the opposite: Everything is in a state of decline, starting good, but getting worse and worse.

The ancient Greeks were perhaps the first to speak of a Golden Age, which was followed by the Silver Age, then the less-glittery Bronze Age, and then our drab Iron Age. The distant past, so the Greeks thought, was a time of superhuman heroes, and we have been degenerating ever since. Darwinism and other modernist ideologies, such as Marxism, would have us believe our Golden Age is yet to come—that we are evolving toward it—but still today we often think of the past with nostalgia, as if a valuable time in our history has been lost and can never be regained. We do this when we compare today's politicians with the founders of our nation—Washington, Jefferson, Madison. Or when we contrast our easygoing, seemingly less-holy church of today to the early church, with its saints willing to die for their faith. Now, it is true that political conflict nearly rent apart eighteenth-century America, and that heresy and petty squabbles plagued the early church, and that the people who lived in what we think of as Golden Ages tended not to consider themselves to be so privileged. Yet the problems they faced do not diminish their standing in our eyes, nor should they.

The beginnings of a venture usually are the times of greatest accomplishment. This is certainly true of new artistic styles, where the beginnings of a new genre usually show the highest creativity. Were there any Greek writers or storytellers who were greater than their very first, Homer, who appeared seemingly from nowhere, as in the myth of Athena, springing up from her father's brain already fully grown and clad in armor? Think of Shakespeare and the other Renaissance dramatists in the very infancy of modern theater, or the English novel in the nineteenth century just decades after the genre was invented, or the early Romantic poets as compared to the later ones. The principle that the early artists in a genre tend to be the best seems to hold true for different styles in painting and even for popular forms such as situational comedies and the various sub-genres of rock 'n' roll. The inventors of a style show the most innovation and creative energy. Their followers may also demonstrate genius, but after a while imitators take over, and the style is reduced to a set of lifeless conventions.

More deeply, the legend of the Golden Age articulates a sense of loss that seems to be part of the human condition. According to the Greek myth, the Golden Age was lost when Pandora opened that forbidden box, which let out all miseries into the world. For Christians, the true Golden Age ended with the fall. But thankfully, though Eden was lost to sin, we have a new paradise to look forward to through the redemption of Christ.

THE LIMITS OF THE PAST

Therefore, Peter, Susan, Edmund, and Lucy—hungry, confused, and lost—must have found it strange to hear in the dwarf's story that they were the embodiment of Narnia's Golden Age. They probably had never thought of themselves in that manner, at least not since they had been back to their own world. But here they are, in Narnia's Age of Iron, with the task of making it Golden again.

Lewis is not necessarily saying that we must seek to re-create the Golden Ages of our past, for that would be impossible. And nor would we want to, because the past had troubles of its own. But this is precisely *why* we must go back—to learn from both the mistakes and the accomplishments of the past and so improve the future.

There is, however, a danger in idealizing the past by thinking that if we could just go back to the way things were all would be well. When Prince Caspian joins the Old Narnia resistance, he is startled to learn that what he thought of as a Golden Age had not only heroes but monsters as well. In their counsels, some of the dwarfs want to enlist the aid of Ogres and Hags. "It gave Caspian a shock to realise that the horrible creatures out of the old stories, as well as the nice ones, had some descendants in Narnia still."[2]

Similarly, the Old West had its virtues, but it also had its monsters—plagues, superstition, and political oppression. The answer to the problems of modernity is not just to retreat into a reactionary past, and Lewis was careful to make that clear. For Lewis, the value of reading old books was *not* that the past was better, but that old books free us from the limited perspective of our own time. He said:

> Every age has its own outlook. It is specially good at seeing certain truths and specially liable to make certain mistakes. We all, therefore, need the books that will correct the characteristic mistakes of our own period. And that means the old books…. Not, of course, that there is any magic about the past. People were no cleverer then than they are now; they made as many mistakes as we. But not the same mistakes. They will not flatter us in the errors we are already committing; and their own errors, being now open and palpable, will not endanger us. Two heads are better than one, not because either is infallible, but because they are unlikely to go wrong in the same direction. To be sure, the books of the future would be just as good a corrective as the books of the past, but unfortunately we cannot get at them.[3]

The solution to the problems of modernity is not to return to castles and feudalism. We cannot solve the problems of today's church by bringing back the early church, with its togas, catacombs, and lions in the Coliseum. It is not possible, nor even desirable, to solve our national problems by reverting to the early days of our republic, which, however heroic, were also times of slavery and strife.

But we are still able to learn from those times. We can learn from them different lessons that might be hidden from our culture today. The founders of our country can serve as examples of political wisdom and selfless statesmanship. Medieval writers can show us fragmented postmodernists what it is like to believe that all of existence has meaning. The early church can teach today's Christians how to respond to a hostile culture—not by conforming to it, but by enduring it with a faith that can win over its persecutors.

A habit of reading old books, Lewis says, can help us transcend the limits of any one particular time and place, including the one we inhabit. That might enable us, to some degree, to bring treasures from the past into our own times, resulting, ironically, in something new, much how the rediscovery of ancient Greece led to a cultural Renaissance throughout Europe. This type of "restoration" has to do less with actually restoring an older culture and more with instilling a larger, less-restricted vision of reality.

In *Prince Caspian*, it is not just the New Narnians, but the Old Narnians as well, who must learn that God is greater than their own limited perspectives and narrow minds.

THE KEY TO C. S. LEWIS

Soon after he became a Christian, Lewis wrote a curious book entitled *Pilgrim's Regress*.[4] Not *Pilgrim's Progress*, John Bunyan's classic tale symbolizing the journey of the Christian life. The kind of "progress" Bunyan referred to was an old word for walking forward. But Lewis describes his spiritual journey as the opposite of a "progress." He experienced a "regress."

The book, like Bunyan's, is an allegory. An everyman-type character named John leaves his childhood home in Puritania, bridling against its rules and restrictions, just as Lewis left behind his Northern Ireland Protestant upbringing. John falls in with Bunyanesque characters like Mr. Sensible and Mr. Humanist. He journeys through the realms of the different philosophies that Lewis had tried to live by (Idealism, Monism, etc.). The story also deals with his temptations, such as lust (the Brown Girls) and worldliness (the Clevers). John is motivated, though, by an ineffable transcendent desire, an experience that breaks in upon him at unexpected times and propels him forward, yearning to find some satisfaction, the nature of which he does not understand.

The best gloss on *Pilgrim's Regress* is Lewis's memoir *Surprised by Joy*, in which he writes of these desires, his early life, and his intellectual and spiritual development through the books he reads, all of which finally culminate in his conversion to Christ. But *Pilgrim's Regress* is both more detailed and more universalized, dealing with other alternatives to Christianity that threw off many people in the early twentieth century, from Marxism to Freudianism.

With intimations of grace and the mysterious leadership of the "Man" (Christ), John comes to accept the Landlord (God) and is received by Mother Kirk (the church). He must navigate the narrow path along the arid rocks on the North (symbolizing rationalism) and the other extreme of the fetid swamps on the South (symbolizing emotionalism). He finds himself regressing, or traveling backward through all of the different realms and ideas he had passed through, which, thanks to his Christian faith, he now understands in a new light. He ends where he began, with the faith of his childhood in Puritania, which he now sees was not about rules and restrictions at all, but grace and faith. He then, like Bunyan, crosses the waters into the everlasting life beyond.

Pilgrim's Regress is an odd book for many people, but it has always been one of my favorites. Its deft portrayals of different philosophies and worldviews are insightful and illuminating. More than that, the book is an evocative fantasy—with giants, dragons, and adventure—of the sort that Lewis later would develop so thoroughly in The Chronicles of Narnia. But most important of all, *Pilgrim's Regress* is something of a key to all of Lewis's later works and to what he was trying to achieve as a writer and as a thinker. Everything that Lewis would write is summed up in the subtitle of *Pilgrim's Regress:* "An Allegorical Apology for Christianity, Reason, and Romanticism."

The phrase seems strange. The words do not seem to go together. Are not Reason and Romanticism opposites? The Enlightenment's Age of Reason was countered, at least for a while, by Romanticism's Age of Emotion. And both movements in their own way opposed Christianity. Those on the side of reason typically considered Christianity's insistence on supernatural doctrines and the ineffable state of the soul nonrational, subjective, and emotional. Romantics, on the other hand, considered Christianity to be *too* rational, with its objective dogmas, its systematic theology, and its subordination of individual experience to the teaching of the church. How can anyone write an "apology" for, which is to say a defense of, *all three* of these contending positions?

Ironically, all three *need* to be defended, since all three are now under attack.

Modernity *began* as the Age of Reason but soon mutated into the Age of Empirical Evidence. Finding truth by means of inductive experiments is not at all the same as finding truth by means of logical analysis. And now that we have slipped into the postmodern era, reason—which presupposes knowable, absolute objective truth—is thrown out altogether.

Romanticism, too, is under attack. The nineteenth-century Romantics took their name from "romantic" medieval tales of knighthood, love, and magic, which we now call fantasies. Yes, the nineteenth-century Romantics cultivated emotion, the inner life, and expressions of the self, but at least in the beginning these all had a transcendent flavor, having to do with a sense of wonder and meaning, an experience in which, as Wordsworth says, "we see into the life of things."[5] The early Romantics were reacting against Enlightenment reason, which seemed to reduce nature to a machine and life to a proposition—that cold, unfeeling mind-set in which, again quoting Wordsworth, "we murder to dissect."[6] But today, even more so than in the 1930s when Lewis wrote this book, this kind of Romanticism is all but lost, reduced to a crude pursuit of physical pleasures and self-aggrandizement. Strictly speaking, the modernity of the twentieth century has lost *both* reason *and* Romanticism. And this is even more true of the postmodern culture of the twenty-first century.

A contemporary of Lewis, T. S. Eliot, wrote about what he called "the dissociation of sensibility" that characterizes the modern condition. Today, he said, thought and feeling are seen as opposites, both going off in different directions, incompatible with each other. Our ideas are in conflict with our emotions or, perhaps worse, have no relationship to each other. But there was a time when thought and feeling went together. Writers from Dante to Shakespeare to metaphysical poets such as John Donne could, in Eliot's words, "feel their thought."[7] Those poets of Old Europe had a "unification of sensibility,"[8] but then a "dissociation of sensibility set in, from which we have never recovered."[9]

Eliot, as a poet trying to unify his own sensibility, came to realize what Dante, Shakespeare, Donne, and Old Europe had in common: Christianity. Indeed, Christianity had provided the wholeness of mind and heart that he yearned for. Eliot shocked his cutting-edge modernist colleagues when he announced his conversion.

Lewis could not stand Eliot's poetry[10]—he disliked intensely its obscurity, darkness, and free verse, and he resented Eliot for setting a style so contrary to his own "golden" verse—but the subtitle to *Pilgrim's Regress* shows that they were wrestling with the same issues and regressing to the same place.

Christianity offers not only a worldview but also a "sensibility," a way to think and to feel. It is so vast and comprehensive that it embraces the intellect and the heart, accounting for both objective truth and subjective experience. Christianity asserts both nature and supernature, matter and spirit. The Christian can experience both clarity and mystery, conviction and wonder.

Lewis is an "apologist," that is, he defends the truth of Christianity. Many readers marvel at the way he uses logic and lucid reasoning to make the case for the Christian faith. Many modernists, both Christian and non-Christian, assume that faith is just a matter of individual experience and are stunned to confront the objective truth of its doctrines. But Lewis also appeals to the heart. He stirs up the imagination to help us realize that our existence is not bound by narrow materialism but is charged with eternal meaning. He is an apologist for Reason, Romanticism, and what holds them together—Christianity.

Defending "Reason, Romanticism, and Christianity" was Lewis's main goal in all of his works, nonfiction as well as fiction. And restoring this Christian sensibility is exactly what he achieved. This is the kind of "regress" Lewis was after in his depiction of the Narnians' efforts to return to their ancient customs. Not some reactionary cultural scheme, but a restoration of the wholeness of heart and mind that can only be found through Jesus Christ.

STUDY QUESTIONS

1. Lewis advocates that we remember the past so that we can learn from both its triumphs and its failures. What are some of the lessons you carry with you from your own past? What can you do to ensure you don't forget them as you move forward?

2. Lewis is defending "Reason, Romanticism, and Christianity." How are each of these under attack today? Why do people see them as incompatible? How can you work to reconcile all three in your daily life?

3. Lewis talks about the value of reading old books. He says that doing so frees us from the limited perspective of our own time. Are you currently reading any old books? If so, what are they? If not, make a list of some you would like to and get started! If you're interested, start a reading group with those whose opinions you trust.

4. T. S. Eliot believed that our post-Enlightenment worldview creates a "dissociation of sensibility" in which our thoughts and our feelings and other parts of our lives go in different directions. In what ways do you compartmentalize your faith from other areas in your life? What can you do to change that?

Four
COMPARTMENTALIZING FAITH: DO YOU BELIEVE IN LIONS?

"I have no use for magic lions which are talking lions and don't talk, and friendly lions though they don't do us any good, and whopping big lions though nobody can see them. It's all bilge and beanstalks as far as I can see."

—Trumpkin, chapter 11

One of the most significant and defining characteristics of modern Narnia is its atheism. Under the harsh rule of King Miraz, most of Narnia has all but forgotten the love and sacrifice of the great lion, Aslan. Lions, according to the Telmarine educational system, do not exist, and this worldview manifests itself throughout Narnian culture. Not surprisingly, even the Old Narnians have fallen into this trap. Not many believe in Aslan anymore, and the ones who do, like Trufflehunter, find it difficult to live out their faith.

Unfortunately, this is also true of the world that we live in. Even though relatively few people deny the existence of any kind of deity altogether, we live in a culture that is now defined by what is called "practical atheism." This is to say that even those who believe in some sort of god, including those who profess faith in the God of the Bible and His Son Jesus, are living as if God does not exist.

For example, some politicians devoutly affirm their religiosity but insist that they will not allow those personal beliefs to affect how they conduct their office. For most of us today, that kind of compartmentalization comes naturally. Our religious beliefs give us some kind of therapeutic benefit, so we hold on to them and internalize them. Our "external" beliefs, though, remain tainted by the culture around us; science, our peers, and the entertainment industry all affect how we act in the real world. We might have a few mystical experiences, but then we have to get practical.

For many of us in this mind-set, the external world either consumes us or loses all meaning for us. Therefore we begin to seek meaning from our own inner feelings. This meaning, however, is by its very nature subjective, experiential, and nonrational. We may still tolerate Christian doctrines, or we may not, but ultimately what's important is the spiritual jolt that Christianity can provide—it's a means to an end. But when it comes to "real life," we are often just as pragmatic as nonbelievers, following our own self-interests or whatever cultural convention is popular at the time.

Even those of us with stronger faith often act as if God is not part of our daily lives. We might consult God on some of the smaller decisions we face, and we might even pray occasionally for safety, encouragement, or for our friends. But when it comes to the larger decisions in life, like our moral beliefs and the way we treat others, we often act out of our own selfish impulses without taking God into account. So even "believers" in God can nevertheless become practical atheists.

Nancy Pearcey, in her book *Total Truth*,[1] explored how both our culture and the church itself have consigned Christianity into the realm of private, interior experience, draining the external world of all spirituality. But consigning God and all that goes with Him into our own personal spheres is not just a theological mistake; it has profound consequences for our culture. For example, if a foreigner visited us from another country, he would see our television, movies, schools, and news media and have no idea that our country was founded on Christian values, or even that we had any religious beliefs at all.

Belief in God once shaped Western culture, forming its assumptions about individual rights, the value of human life, the sanctity of the family, and so on.[2] But how can we retain these things after we have jettisoned their foundation? God is now a cultural exile. So how can those who believe in Him function amid those who do not? And how can they persuade the unbelievers that He is real after all?

SECULARIST NARNIA

In modern Narnia, atheism is mandatory, as we can see from King Miraz's treatment of his nephew, Prince Caspian. Upon learning that Caspian's nurse has encouraged him to take interest in the stories of Old Narnia, Miraz becomes enraged. The king has gone to great lengths to create a sense of fear in his subjects concerning all things spiritual, and he is not about to allow the imagination of a young boy to jeopardize his crown. At one point he even shouts to Caspian, "Never let me catch you talking—or *thinking*, either—about all those silly stories again."[3]

But the thing about God is that He never really goes away and that He tends to make Himself known. So it is not surprising that Prince Caspian's nurse is soon replaced by a tutor named Dr. Cornelius, who, unbeknownst to King Miraz, is steeped in knowledge about Old Narnia and the myth of Aslan. Like many of us today, Dr. Cornelius is not even sure that he believes in all those old stories, but he still speaks of a strange yearning in his heart, even though he has experienced nothing that can prove beyond doubt the existence of dwarfs or fauns or great talking lions. He has seen some things over the years that he can't explain—never enough to know for sure, of course, but sufficient to keep hope alive that there might be something more.

Dr. Cornelius was giving voice to what another historical scholar—C. S. Lewis—felt in his days of unbelief. In his autobiography, *Surprised by Joy*, Lewis describes how he fell in with the casual atheism of the modern world. And yet, throughout his life, he recounts how he would experience what he calls stabs of "joy," or more precisely a mixture of joy with ineffable longing.[4] This experience was always unexpected and could come upon him at any time: perhaps through illustrations in a Beatrix Potter children's book, or by listening to Wagner's *Ride of the Valkyries*, or by reading a George MacDonald fairy tale. The experiences were outside his control, and he could never cause them to come back again on his own.

Mere longing, of course, does not prove anything—whether the existence of God or of Old Narnia—but rather, these moments of joy were fleeting glimpses of transcendence. Lewis, even while he was an atheist, had the sense that these fleeting experiences were foretastes of a meaning that lay beyond the world he knew. The pilgrim in *Pilgrim's Regress* had visions of mysterious islands that he yearned to reach, visions that kept him searching on his path. When Lewis finally became a Christian, he realized that those moments of joy he had been experiencing were signs of a supernatural reality beyond this life, pointing ultimately to God and to Lewis's true home in heaven.

But Dr. Cornelius, who doubts the existence of dwarfs even though he is himself part dwarf, also makes another point about New Narnia and its institutionalized secularism. When he mentions that the ruins of the palace Cair Paravel were thought to be at the mouth of the Great River by the sea, Prince Caspian is horrified. Those are the Black Woods! They are haunted! Everyone is afraid to go there! "Your Highness speaks as you have been taught," replies Dr. Cornelius, "but it is all lies."[5]

False worldviews indeed are "taught," not just in modern Narnia but in our world as well. Just as in Narnia, God-excluding secularism is promulgated in our schools, our media, and our culture. But why? Dr. Cornelius gives the answer: The Telmarines fear the sea because, according to the old stories, Aslan comes from over the sea. They also fear the woods because of their quarrel with the trees. "They feel safer if no one in Narnia dares to go down to the coast and look out to the sea—toward Aslan's land and the morning and the eastern end of the world."[6]

A major reason many people do not believe in God is fear, fear that perhaps there *is* a God to whom they are accountable. According to the Bible, the real reason for unbelief is not intellectual argumentation, emotional struggles with the problem of evil, or even historical shifts in worldview, though these are prominent rationalizations for lack of faith. Rather, on the deepest level, the reason for unbelief is *sin*. Paul tells us in Romans, "For the wrath of God is revealed from heaven against all ungodliness and unrighteousness of men, who by their unrighteousness suppress the truth" (1:18).

Unrighteousness has a way of suppressing truth, and we all know why. We like our sin, and we want to keep doing it, whether consciously or subconsciously. Therefore we would much rather justify our behavior and deny any wrongdoing than repent and accept Christ's forgiveness. We can do that by denying God's moral law, and the easiest way of doing that is by denying that God exists. If there is no God, then there is no one to judge us. We can do whatever we want. Of course, if there *is* a God, then we're in trouble, so we have to fight the very concept of God. We have to find arguments to protect ourselves, to defend ourselves against evidence to the contrary. Furthermore, because we are so personally invested in the nonexistence of God, people who do believe in Him make us angry. They touch a nerve. We are happier when we don't even have to think about religious issues, so like the Telmarines we just "don't go there."

But the apostle Paul tells us that this is a useless exercise, because the people who *say* they do not believe in God actually, deep down, do know He exists:

> For what can be known about God is plain to
> them, because God has shown it to them. For his

> invisible attributes, namely, his eternal power and
> divine nature, have been clearly perceived, ever
> since the creation of the world, in the things that
> have been made. So they are without excuse. For
> although they knew God, they did not honor him
> as God or give thanks to him, but they became
> futile in their thinking, and their foolish hearts
> were darkened. (Rom. 1:19–21)

People do not reject God out of ignorance. It isn't that they haven't heard of Him or have otherwise been blinded to His existence. They know what they are doing, but they "suppress" the truth and keep it out of their consciousness. Of course, the next step after denial of what we know to be true is to construct something that we like better, something that won't challenge us. According to Romans, this is exactly what happened: "Claiming to be wise, they became fools, and exchanged the glory of the immortal God for images resembling mortal man and birds and animals and creeping things" (Rom. 1:22–23). Whereupon, God chose to punish us in a most horrible fashion, by "giving us up" to our sinful desires; that is, He allows us to do what we want (see Rom. 1:24–32).

Sin leads to the rejection of God, which, in turn, leads to even more sin. This vicious cycle, in which none of us have an excuse (see Rom. 2), is broken only by the undeserved grace of God and His free gift of redemption through Jesus Christ. "For all have sinned and fall short of the glory of God, and are justified by his grace as a gift, through the redemption that is in Christ Jesus, whom God put forward as a propitiation by his blood, to be received by faith" (Rom. 3:23–25).

Though C. S. Lewis was a great proponent for the existence of God and the truth of Christianity, he knew that the ultimate answer to atheism, both overt and implicit, is grace, redemption, and faith; or in other words, the gospel of Jesus Christ. As we will see in chapter 10, Aslan teaches Narnians to believe in lions again not by winning them over in an argument but by bounding into their lives and leading them in a joyous "romp" of freedom, love, and new life.

CONSERVATIVE ATHEISM

But as I mentioned earlier, King Miraz and the Telmarines are not the only atheists in Narnia. Trumpkin, the dwarf who has been narrating the story to Peter, Susan, Edmund, and Lucy, does not believe in God either. This is surprising, though, because in many ways Trumpkin is fighting for the same cause as Prince Caspian and the Pevensie children: to cast off the evil rule of King Miraz and restore Narnia to its rightful order. But unlike Dr. Cornelius, whose sense of Old Narnia is built on myth and legend, Trumpkin can clearly see the world around him. He speaks daily with other dwarfs and talking animals, and he knows of the ruins of Cair Paravel and the great altar where Aslan was slain—yet these truths have no effect on him.

Trumpkin's is a commonsense kind of atheism, similar to that of Lewis's own tutor, William T. Kirkpatrick, the "Old Knock" affectionately referred to in *Surprised by Joy*.[7] Trumpkin simply cannot believe in what he cannot see or touch or feel. He is a dwarf of integrity, not needing to believe in Aslan to do what is right.[8] This is difficult for Caspian and the others to understand, since for them, who have never experienced the world of Old Narnia, the mere existence of dwarfs and ogres and other talking animals is proof enough to believe in Aslan. Prince Caspian put it best, "The people who laughed at Aslan would have laughed at stories of Talking Beasts and Dwarfs."[9]

Of course, Christians who get involved in politics are often surprised to find that the people fighting on their side are sometimes unbelievers. Some conservatives are followers of Ayn Rand, the "objectivist" who rejected the existence of God, condemned Christianity for helping the weak, and championed "the virtue of selfishness."[10] Her philosophy translated into libertarian laws, free-market economics, and distrust of big government—all major conservative causes of interest to many Christians.

In fact, many political conservatives have quite "liberal" moral values when it comes to issues like fidelity in marriage, substance abuse, and even abortion. And conversely, many theologically and morally conservative Christians firmly plant themselves on the liberal side of the political aisle. Clearly Christians are right to engage in the issues of their time, and when they do so, they may find themselves fighting alongside unexpected allies. In World War II, America and the communist Soviet Union cooperated in fighting Nazi Germany, their common enemy. Christian activists have joined with feminists to battle pornography and sex trafficking. Evangelicals, Catholics, Mormons, and Muslims can march together in front of abortion clinics. As long as we do not compromise our faith or the integrity of our worship, there is nothing wrong with working alongside those of other beliefs to advance a common cause.

Surely a major aspect of the Christian faith is the effect it has on the world around us, for we are called to feed and clothe the poor and care for the widows. But political issues and social agendas are not really at the heart of why Christ came and died. God is in the business of changing hearts, of restoring us to our proper place in creation—at His right hand. Sometimes wars, cultural or otherwise, may need to be fought, but they have to do with this world that passes away, not the kingdom of heaven.

Trumpkin, as with many atheists, seems to miss the point of who or what kind of thing God even is—whether He exists or not. The dwarf is condescending toward believers. He tells Lucy, who has seen Aslan, that she probably just saw a regular lion and that the lion she knew thousands of years ago would be pretty elderly by now. Trumpkin has rather childish reference points in thinking about God. He says that, even if a lion could have lived so long, he would probably have lost his speech and gone wild like all of the other talking animals. He has no conception that Aslan is of a different order of being entirely.

In fact, Trumpkin's thoughts about God are much like those of the popular astrophysicist Carl Sagan. He once criticized the account of Christ's ascension, saying that, if Jesus blasted off from Earth and was able to travel at the fastest velocity in the universe by reaching the speed of light, He still would not have reached heaven after all these years. He would simply be two thousand light-years away from Earth. Though Sagan could comprehend the complexities of quantum physics (much like Trumpkin having an understanding of his own world), he conceived of the God he did not believe in as some sort of giant alien living just outside the cosmos. He then ridicules such a deity and the people ignorant enough to believe in such a thing—even though that is *not* how believers conceive of God. In reality, we know God to be a spiritual being who fills the universe with His presence, He is the one "in [whom] we live and move and have our being" (Acts 17:28). So how can people like Trumpkin or Carl Sagan, who are clueless about religion, ever come to believe in God? For them the issue is not simply believing in the existence of a god—the issue is actually *believing God*, or, rather, coming to faith. Rational arguments about the existence of God or of the truth of Christian doctrine can be helpful, as Lewis demonstrates in his apologetic works. But God is not an abstract idea to be debated; He is a reality to be encountered, a Person who makes Himself known.

Trumpkin and others like him will never rationalize themselves to the existence of God. Like Thomas and so many others throughout history, they have to stick their fingers in His side in order to believe. The lion will have to pounce on them. They—and all of us—need to feel the weight of his paw and heat of his breath.

STUDY QUESTIONS

1. "Practical atheism" means holding a belief in God but acting in daily life as though He does not exist. In what ways are you guilty of practical atheism? What can you do to change how you act on your beliefs in real life?

2. What are some things you have seen or felt over the years that you can't explain but have given you hope that there might be something more out there? Why is it sometimes hard to remember these things when we're struggling in our faith?

3. What are some of the things you fear when it comes to your relationship with God? How do these fears keep you from drawing close to Him?

4. What are some idols you have constructed to take the place of God in your life? (Be honest!) What can you do about them right now?

5. What would it mean for you to experience the "weight of his paw and heat of his breath"? How could you use this experience to witness to others? How would that be different from using a rational argument? Which do you think would be more effective and why?

Five
FAITH: WALKING NOT BY SIGHT

And so at last they got on the move. Lucy went first,
biting her lip and trying not to say all the things she
thought of saying to Susan. But she forgot them when
she fixed her eyes on Aslan. He turned and walked at
a slow pace about thirty yards ahead of them. The
others had only Lucy's directions to guide them.

—chapter 11

So where has Aslan been all these years anyway? If the New Narnians do not believe in lions, they surely have good reason. They have never seen one before. Similarly, God seems suspiciously absent from the modern and postmodern world. True, people believed in God in the past, and under His influence they even achieved some great things. But it's easy to believe when angels wrestle you to the ground and giant pillars of fire guide your way in dark places. In an age of unbelief, though, how can any of us maintain belief on our own?

God does not simply ask that we believe in His existence. For many people, that is easy enough. Rather, God wants us to trust Him. Which is to say, we must have faith.

For most people that seems harder than simply believing He exists. But faith is actually not hard at all. Faith comes when God reveals Himself to us. He has done that by coming to us in a tangible way—not as an abstract idea to be mentally comprehended and assented to, but by becoming a Man. God entered our lives by assuming the burden of human flesh in the person of Jesus Christ. And what's more, though He lived a sinless life, He accepted the penalty for our own sins by dying on the cross and, in doing so, passed on the reward for His own goodness to us. To accept this— to trust the sacrifice of Christ as the basis of salvation rather than our own works—is to be justified by faith.

This was the theme of the first Narnia book, *The Lion, the Witch and the Wardrobe*, in which Aslan died for the sinful deeds of Edmund and then rose again. The second Narnia book, *Prince Caspian,* dramatizes what it means to *walk* by faith—to live one's life and to fight one's battles according to that faith. But many things can distract us along the way.

FAITH IN ONESELF

After Peter, Susan, Edmund, and Lucy hear Trumpkin's story, which culminates in the Old Narnians sounding Queen Susan's horn, they realize they have been summoned into Narnia to help Prince Caspian as he leads the resistance against Miraz and his Telmarines. But first they must travel to Aslan's How—the site of Aslan's original sacrifice. Little do they know that this seemingly easy hike will quickly become a journey of faith.

They set out on the two-day journey to the place Aslan was slain, but the woods are thick and the old landmarks have disappeared. They often follow what they think are paths through the woods but that end suddenly. It's not long before they feel completely lost.

At one point they come to the edge of a precipice overlooking a river. On the other side of the gorge is an even higher cliff. They debate whether this might be the River Rush, which has carved out a canyon after so many years and which might lead them to Aslan's How. As the children and the dwarf try to figure out which way to go, Lucy catches a glimpse of Aslan.

It might have seemed like one of Dr. Cornelius's glimpses of a faun—uncertain and far away—or like one of C. S. Lewis's ineffable experiences of transcendent joy. But Lucy is certain that she saw the lion, at a distance, far up into the rocks. The problem is that Lucy is the only one who saw him, and being the youngest, nobody takes her seriously. The others do not believe her. Peter asks her where she thinks she saw him. Lucy bristles, "Don't talk like a grownup. I didn't *think* I saw him, I saw him."[1] (Notice how Lewis understands children. They *hate* for adults to talk down to them.)

This scene captures the loneliness of faith. It can sometimes be difficult to be convinced of the reality of God in the midst of people who are oblivious to His existence. Peer pressure can force people to deny what they really believe. Though parents lament its effect on children, peer pressure is probably even more of a problem for adults. Furthermore, a particular individual's religious experience is hardly strong evidence. The individual may be mistaken or deluded or hallucinatory. But Lucy knows Aslan when she sees him. She clings to her belief—which is to say, she has faith—no matter what.

Trumpkin, with his commonsense skepticism, tries to reason with her. Maybe she did see a lion, but how did she know it was this *talking* lion, Aslan? Most of the animals have lost their former gift of language and gone wild. Besides, Aslan would be pretty old by now, as it was 1,288 years since she had last seen him.

But Lucy holds on to her faith. She tells her siblings she got the impression—from his face—that Aslan wanted them to follow in his direction. But to the older children, this makes no sense. It would lead them in the opposite direction from where they want to go. They had planned to go down to the river. Aslan's way—if it was Aslan—would require them to climb up the cliff.

The group decides to vote on which way they will go. Susan and Trumpkin make the logical choice—it would be much easier to go downhill, get out of the woods, and follow a path that their minds tell them will take them to their destination. Instead of believing Lucy's testimony and acting in faith, they want to follow their own understandings, trusting the rational results of their own intellects. Isn't this so typical of how we usually conduct our lives? Many of us talk about faith, but when it comes to moral decisions and spiritual convictions, we oftentimes decide based on what makes the most sense, or what "feels right" at the time.

Edmund would have reacted the same way as his older brother and sister, but he remembers that Lucy made a similar claim once before—something concerning a faun and a lamppost inside a wardrobe. No one believed her then, either. Edmund remembers that he had been the worst, teasing and tormenting her, but they all discovered later that she was right. So this time, Edmund decides to have faith in his sister, trusting that what she saw was real, even though it contradicts his own experience.

But Edmund isn't just putting his faith in his sister. Lucy is merely telling the others what she saw—Edmund is putting his faith in what she is giving testimony to. In the same way, back in our world, our faith can grow and be strengthened by the faith of fellow Christians. But we must sometimes be willing to lay down our own desires in order to follow someone we trust.

Ultimately Peter sides with the logical perspective, and the group starts off toward the river, with Lucy following behind, crying. This way, however, though it made the best sense at the time of the decision, turns out to be a disaster. It leads them through brambles, bogs, and chasms. And after an arduous, exhausting journey, they walk into a hail of arrows from Miraz's sentries. Driven back, the children realize that the other path, the way Lucy—and Aslan—had wanted them to go, would have enabled them to pass by all of these obstacles.

The children voted to walk by sight rather than by faith. They put their trust in what they could see—the easy slope down to the river—instead of in Lucy's words about Aslan. This is the same dilemma that we struggle with in our world. Should we trust ourselves and the things we can see with our own eyes? Or should we trust God and what He has to say about the world?

Today, pop psychologists, self-help gurus, and power-of-positive-thinking preachers talk about the importance of "faith." But faith must have an object. What is your faith *in?* Much of today's faith talk is all about having faith in *oneself.* "Trust yourself," we are exhorted. A motivational poster proclaims, "Dare to believe in yourself." Then there is the explicit theological statement that is so common that is has become cliché: "Have faith in yourself."

The notion that the self is the proper object of faith has practically become a religion unto itself, and this teaching is often developed with theological rigor. I found this statement on the Internet: "Living at the edge of faith means that you are willing to take the risk and leap out into your greatness."[2] This alludes to Kierkegaard's "leap of faith,"[3] in which Kierkegaard felt a leap was necessary to accept Christianity because of its inherent paradoxes (e.g., the notion that Jesus could be 100 percent God and 100 percent man at the same time). But in this quote from the Internet this concept is not applied to faith in Christ but to faith in *oneself.* And not only that, but it is also applied to one's "greatness." Indeed, if a person is going to be the object of his own faith, he must think very highly of himself. Ironically, according to the image in this statement, the person who thinks highly of himself is jumping off a cliff!

We have already discussed modernists, who by their so-called progressive philosophies dismiss God from the universe altogether. Postmodernists, though, take another approach to God. In postmodernism, such a high importance is placed on subjective truth and "feeling" that in effect people become gods unto themselves. The modernists who believed the material world is all there is denied that there is any such thing as a Creator, a Lawgiver, or a God. But if, as the postmodernists say, truth is a "construction," then truth *does* have a creator. And that creator is each of *us.* And if morality is also a "construction," based on what the majority of people believes at any given moment, then we do have a lawgiver: *ourselves*. And thus, according to the postmodernist worldview, each individual becomes his own god. Thus is fulfilled Satan's promise in the garden: "You will be like God" (Gen. 3:5).

Lewis's *Discarded Image* is a scholarly study of the old cosmology that assumed the earth was the center of the universe, around which the moon, sun, planets, and stars revolved in celestial spheres. Postmodernists, ironically, have in a sense reverted to that same model. Humanity is once again the center of the universe.

This self-divinization is the antithesis of Christianity. To be a Christian means we must *stop* having faith in ourselves—in how good we are or in how much we know—and acknowledge instead our failures, our loneliness, and our sinfulness. We must instead place our faith in Jesus Christ, who has come to save us.

THE CALL TO FAITH

And so, faith in Christ is bigger than faith in oneself. And it is also bigger than faith in faith, as some have tried to reduce it to, as if the basis of salvation had something to do with the quality or intensity of one's faith. Christian faith has to do with trusting in something and someone outside ourselves: Jesus was actually nailed to a cross for sins He didn't commit. He died for us, and He rose from death in victory. Our faith must not be in what goes on inside our heads, but in the objective work of Christ.

When we have faith in *ourselves*—in our own reasoning, our own desires and choices, the way *we* want to go—we encounter only brambles, mire, ambushes, and dead ends. Instead, like Lucy following Aslan, we must have faith in Christ and in the way He wants us to go. In this way, faith is not the same as knowledge. Neither is faith the same as experience. Peter, Susan, Edmund, and Trumpkin do not see Aslan. Only Lucy does. But somehow the others need to have faith in Lucy's words about Aslan.

First, though, the story dramatizes the nature of Lucy's faith. That night, while everyone is sleeping, Lucy hears a voice calling her name. She goes out into the darkness. As she walks through the woods, the trees seem to be dancing. In the midst of it all, she sees Aslan and runs to him.

Again, genuine faith involves a relationship with someone outside of ourselves. Aslan here is "other" than Lucy. He is no abstract proposition. Rather, he is incarnate, tangible, and objectively present. Just as Christ was truly man, Aslan is truly lion. Lucy buries her face in his mane. He licks her nose. And in a vivid sensory description symbolic of the Holy Spirit, "His warm breath came all around her" (cf. John 20:22).[4]

Furthermore, Aslan *calls* her by name. Theologically, Christ, through His Word, calls us to Himself, and this is the beginning of our faith. "Those whom he called he also justified" (Rom. 8:30). The description of Lucy hearing and following Aslan is evocative of Christ's own words speaking of Himself as the Good Shepherd: "When he has brought out all his own, he goes before them, and the sheep follow him, for they know his voice" (John 10:4).

Lucy remarks that Aslan is bigger than when she knew him before. Aslan replies that this is because she is older. "Every year you grow, you will find me bigger."5 The more one matures in faith, the greater God appears.

In the presence of holiness, the sense of our own righteousness fades away. Aslan reminds Lucy that she and the others have much to do and have wasted much time. Lucy starts to congratulate herself and condemn the others, but she hears coming from the lion a faint growl. Convicted, she apologizes for being judgmental but cannot help but note how what happened at least was not her fault. Aslan just looks at her. With the self-knowledge that comes from a confrontation with God, Lucy confesses that she *was* at fault, that she should have followed Aslan, even if only by herself. She realizes that if she took the lonely way of faith, she would not have been alone after all, that Aslan would have been with her.

Lucy is at first dismayed that Aslan will not just roar in and defeat their enemies, that he intends to work through them instead. Indeed, it can be a frightful proposition when we are called to something we know we don't have the strength to accomplish in and of ourselves. But Lucy "could feel lion-strength going into her."6

Faith is not just a mental assent. Faith is alive. It grows and bears fruit. When we have faith in Christ, He lives in and through us. Faith changes us on the inside and manifests itself in righteous actions that we perform freely and that He performs through us. "Now you are a lioness," Aslan tells Lucy. "And now all Narnia will be renewed."7

THE IMPORTANCE OF WALKING

But what about the others? They do not have the direct experience with Aslan that Lucy has. A little later in the story Lucy tries to convince them again that Aslan is standing in their presence, but Peter and Susan, unable to see him, just roll their eyes. Peter, playing the rationalist, cannot understand why Aslan would not appear to the rest of them like he used to. Susan plays the grown-up and simply scolds Lucy for playing games. Lucy, though, will not back down, even to the point of threatening to follow Aslan alone if the others will not join her.

Significantly, Edmund believes and follows Aslan on Lucy's authority. Peter and Susan also follow her reluctantly, arguing and sulking. But Lucy "fixed her eyes on Aslan."[8] This recalls, of course, Hebrews 12:2: "looking to Jesus, the founder and perfector of our faith." As they make their way through the darkness, "Lucy had her eyes on the Lion and the rest had their eyes on Lucy."[9]

At one point, it looks as though they are about to be led right off a cliff, but then they see a path before them. Gradually, Edmund makes out Aslan's shadow, and soon enough he can see the lion himself. Notice how because Edmund was one of the first to follow Lucy, he is also one of the first to see Aslan. This is no coincidence, and here is a powerful spiritual truth that Lewis refers to in some of his other writings as well: Our faith is strengthened as we walk in it. In *Mere Christianity* he wrote:

> Do not waste time bothering whether you "love" your neighbor; act as if you did. As soon as we do this we find one of the greatest secrets. When you are behaving as if you loved someone, you will presently come to love him. If you injure someone

you dislike, you will find yourself disliking him
more. If you do him a good turn, you will find
yourself disliking him less.[10]

Here he is speaking directly about charity, but he is also speaking indirectly about faith in general. The more we walk in our faith,
the stronger it will become. This is why Peter and Susan, after walking solely on the basis of trust alone, eventually are able to see Aslan
for themselves.

Finally, when they reach the Stone Table, the place of sacrifice
and redemption, the children are all able to see Aslan clearly and
come to him. Aslan commends Edmund, who followed him out of
sheer faith. Peter confesses he had been leading everyone wrong.
And Susan admits that deep down she did believe Lucy was telling
the truth and that Aslan was really there, but that she had refused
to acknowledge it. Notice how sharp the contrast is between Susan's
experience and Edmund's: Edmund is willing to act on his belief,
though he is unsure, and soon finds himself being led by the lion.
Susan is less willing to act on the same belief, and so it takes her
much longer to see how Aslan is working. In the end, Aslan ban-
ishes Susan's fears and—in Lewis's description of the Holy
Spirit—breathes on her.

For Edmund, Peter, and Susan, this journey in the dark, led
by someone they could not see, following only the testimony of
someone they trust, dramatizes the nature of faith. According to
the book of Hebrews, "faith is the assurance of things hoped for,
the conviction of things not seen" (11:1). The children who follow
Aslan without being able to see him, on trust alone, exemplify

what was said by the apostle Paul: "We walk by faith, not by sight" (2 Cor. 5:7).

THE IMPORTANCE OF HEARING

Lucy, on the other hand, is a parallel to those first disciples who saw Jesus and told others about Him. This is important, because seeing is not always believing. For many, even seeing Jesus in the midst of all His miracles was not enough to create faith. Jesus said to some of those who witnessed His mighty works, "You have seen me and yet do not believe" (John 6:36). Even in the face of undeniable visual evidence, faith remains a gift of God, as our Lord immediately makes clear: "All that the Father gives me will come to me, and whoever comes to me I will never cast out" (John 6:37). Lucy did not merely see—she believed.

But perhaps what's more important is what Lucy did *after* she saw and believed. For those who saw Jesus would play an important role in bringing the rest of us to faith. Luke refers to the sources for his gospel as "those who from the beginning were eyewitnesses and ministers of the word." Those who had seen "the things that have been accomplished among us," in turn, "have delivered them to us" (Luke 1:1–2). We were not there when Jesus lived and died and rose again, but we have the eyewitness testimony recorded in the New Testament. Like Peter, Susan, and Edmund, we are following people who *have* seen Jesus.

But it is much more than that. In His prayer in the garden of Gethsemane, right before His arrest, Jesus prays for His disciples. And then He prays for us: "I do not ask for these only, but also for those who will believe in me through their word" (John 17:20). Their word will be a means of causing others to believe. This is because their word—the apostolic testimony, inspired by the Holy Spirit—would be written down as God's Word. Jesus promised His disciples, "The Holy Spirit, whom the Father will send in my name, he will teach you all things and bring to your remembrance all that I have said to you" (John 14:26).

Ultimately, what creates faith is the Word of God: "Faith comes from hearing, and hearing through the word of Christ" (Rom. 10:17). Hearing, not seeing. Christians have traditionally not put a lot of stock in "visions." It is not necessary to see God. Indeed, a god we can *see* is more likely to be a false god. The word "idol" literally means "image." But we are to *hear* God when He addresses us in His Word. The Word of God is not just information; it has divine power. "For the word of God is living and active, sharper than any two-edged sword, piercing to the division of soul and of spirit, of joints and of marrow, and discerning the thoughts and intentions of the heart" (Heb. 4:12). God's Word convicts us of our sin, assures us of Christ's forgiveness, and calls us to Him. God's Word is a means of grace, connecting us to Christ and carving faith into our hearts.

"Have you believed because you have seen me?" asked the Lord to Thomas, who had to touch Christ's wounds to be convinced of His resurrection. "Blessed are those who have not seen and yet have believed" (John 20:29). Meaning us. We who believe because of God's Word may even have an advantage over those who did see Jesus. I have often reflected that I probably would have been among the skeptics had I been there, refusing to believe my eyes. I am thankful that I have been brought to faith instead through the Word, which has pierced my heart and changed it.

In Narnian terms, Lucy was one of the women in Narnia's Easter story who personally encountered the risen Christ. She was an eye-witness. Edmund was the sinner for whom Aslan specifically died. But he did not witness Aslan's death at the Stone Table, nor was he there when Aslan rose from the dead. He heard of what Aslan did for him, and this changed him forever, from being a selfish, bullying brat to being a loyal brother. But his salvation was accomplished outside of himself. In *Prince Caspian*, Edmund cannot see Aslan, but he walks through the darkness by faith, trusting Lucy's word, which becomes his vehicle for knowing what Aslan would have him do.

Ultimately, faith is not just a walk in the dark. Certainly such times cause us to exercise our faith and thus make it stronger. But the Bible describes faith in terms of "assurance" and "conviction." God's Word and sacraments bring us face-to-face with Christ.

THE IMPORTANCE OF GRACE

But one last thing must be mentioned here concerning the character we have scarcely discussed in this chapter until now: Trumpkin. What happens to him during all this? How were his arguments against the existence of Aslan answered? What must he have felt when he finally met the lion face-to-face?

At the Stone Table, after his reunion with the four children, Aslan summons the "Son of Earth" with a roar. Trembling, the dwarf comes into the presence of the one in whom he refused to believe.

And Aslan, like a cat on a mouse, pounces on him.

The lion carries Trumpkin in his mouth, shakes him, tosses him into the air, and catches him in his velvet paws. "Son of Earth," Aslan asks, "shall we be friends?"

"Ye-he-he-hes," Trumpkin responds, experiencing the power of God for the first time.

Aslan's pouncing is a great symbol for the grace of God. Yes, atheists may need to be intellectually convinced of the existence of God, but even if they are, that comes far short of faith. Apologetics is important, and C. S. Lewis was one of its great practitioners. But ultimately what turns atheists into believers is the grace of God. He works through His Word—the apostolic testimony, the Bible, the preaching of the Word, and our proclamation of that Word when we explain the gospel to others. Lewis's apologetic writings are not just arguments, but are effective proclamations of God's Word. But, ultimately, what turns an unbeliever into a believer, transforming doubt into faith, is the active grace of God. Faith comes when God pounces.

STUDY QUESTIONS

1. How are you doing at walking by faith? By truly living your life and fighting your battles according to your faith in Jesus Christ? (Be honest!) What can you do to go deeper?

2. How are "believing in God" and "believing God" different? How can you better act out your belief in daily life?

3. Martin Luther, in his explanation of the first of the Ten Commandments, in his *Large Catechism,* takes a different approach to the question of God than is usual. He asks, "What does it mean to have a god?" The answer: Your god is the thing you have faith in.

   In this sense, even atheists have a god. If you delve deep, you find that everyone has faith in something. What are some things people put their faith in today? What are some things you put your faith in? How are they misleading substitutes for the one true God?

4. In the story, Aslan says that "every year you grow, you will find me bigger." How big does God seem to you right now? Is He growing in size or staying the same? What can you do differently to start or enhance that growth process?

5. In the story, the Pevensie children have to walk by faith and not by sight. They cannot see where they are going, but they must trust Aslan and follow him. What are some situations in which you too did not have a clear sense of where you were going

or what would happen, but had to walk by faith in Christ? What can you do to strengthen that faith for future unknowns?

6. In the story, only Lucy can see Aslan. Peter, Susan, and Edmund cannot see him, but they trust Lucy. By following her, they are also following Aslan. Who are the people in your life whose spiritual leadership you can trust and who can help you in your walk of faith? How can you show your appreciation for their contribution to your life?

NATURE: OBJECTIVE REALITY

*To sleep under the stars, to drink nothing but well
water and to live chiefly on nuts and wild fruit, was
a strange experience for Caspian after his bed with
silken sheets in a tapestried chamber at the castle,
with meals laid out on gold and silver dishes in the
anteroom, and attendants ready at his call. But he
had never enjoyed himself more. Never had sleep
been more refreshing nor food tasted more savory,
and he began already to harden and his face wore
a kinglier look.*

—chapter 7

According to Lewis, the modern world does not only have a problem with God—it also has a problem with nature. That might
seem odd, since modernists tend to have a high regard for natural
things. But for Lewis, nature is not just wildlife and landscapes
(though he does maintain a certain fondness for these aspects of
nature as well). Nature has to do with objective reality itself. And

that reality is not meaningless at all, despite what people assume today, but rather possesses an objective order and is governed by objective law.

This objective law not only consists of so-called scientific laws, referring to the mathematical consistency of the physical realm, but also includes moral law, which contains certain intrinsic hierarchies and authorities. This is what the classic philosophers and theologians whom Lewis favored called the "natural law."

Unfortunately, Lewis believed, our world has drained all life, meaning, and wonder from the natural order. For instance, Narnia was once filled with talking animals and all sorts of other magical creatures, but in *Prince Caspian* a large portion of these creatures have disappeared. The land seems to have gone "wild," so to speak. Nearly all the animals have lost their gift of speech, except for a very few, and all the old authorities have been overthrown. Thankfully, as you will see, the magic is not completely lost. And Lewis, romantic that he confesses himself to be, seeks to reenchant nature for his readers, to help awaken us again to the wonders of God's created order.

TALKING ANIMALS

Lewis had a lifelong love of animals. And what's more, that love often included an imaginative interest in talking animals, which would become the signature motif of The Chronicles of Narnia.

When Lewis was just six years old, he started writing stories and drawing pictures of an entire imaginary world of his creation, which he called Animal-Land, or Boxen. It was inhabited by dressed animals who could talk. They included King Bunny, Tom and Bob Mouse, and the great hero Sir Ben, who was a frog. With the encouragement of his brother, Warren, young Lewis, who went by the name of "Jack," eventually created a whole history of Boxen, from medieval times to the age of steamships.[1]

What Boxen amounted to was what Lewis's friend J. R. R. Tolkien would later call a "sub-creation," a self-contained fictional universe, whose author is imitating the Creator of the actual universe.[2] Tolkien, of course, was the master of subcreation, with his Middle-earth, as immortalized in *The Hobbit*, *The Lord of the Rings*, *The Silmarillion*, and other associated tales and histories. Lewis's Narnia is also a subcreated world, though Tolkien thought it violated the rules of true fantasy with all of its jumping back and forth between twentieth-century England. Though little Jack Lewis's Boxen was obviously a progenitor of Narnia, the adult Lewis stressed that his Animal-Land was different in an important way: It was a world of steamships, political history, and prosaic everyday life. In a footnote to his account of his childhood in *Surprised by Joy*, Lewis says, "Animal-Land had nothing whatsoever in common with Narnia except the anthropomorphic beasts. Animal-Land, by its whole quality, excluded the least hint of wonder."[3]

And yet, for Lewis, talking animals would forever be connected to wonder, indeed, to those stabs of joy that would play a role in his conversion to Christianity. His brother, Warren, also made up an imaginary world (with the real-life name of India), which Jack eventually tied into Boxen. One day while they were playing, Warren made a toy garden in the lid of a biscuit tin, built with moss, twigs, and flowers. This tiny model of nature, Lewis said in retrospect, "was the first beauty I ever knew. What the real garden had failed to do, the toy garden did. It made me aware of nature—not, indeed, as a storehouse of forms and colors but as something cool, dewy, fresh, exuberant."[4] In terms of our earlier discussion, this childish work of art "defamiliarized" nature for Lewis, opening his eyes to its wonderment for the very first time.

Years later, he stood under a flowering currant bush and suddenly remembered that toy garden. He said he was suddenly overwhelmed with what Milton called "enormous bliss," a powerful desire for something he did not even understand. But then, like Dr. Cornelius's glimpse of a faun, the moment dissolved.

> Before I knew what I desired, the desire itself was gone, the glimpse withdrawn, the world turned commonplace again, or only stirred by a longing for the longing that had just ceased. It had taken only a moment of time; and in a certain sense everything else that had ever happened to me was insignificant in comparison.[5]

This was Lewis's first experience of transcendence—that vision of the island in *Pilgrim's Regress*—and it was occasioned by the conjunction of a real-life plant and an imaginary garden.

The second experience of such joy and longing came when he read a book by the genius of talking animals, Beatrix Potter. Most famous for her story *The Tale of Peter Rabbit*, Potter crafted tiny books that would just fit a child's hand and illustrated them with exquisite watercolors. And the stories were all about talking animals, each of whom was a lively character as well as a realistic animal. In *Surprised by Joy*, Lewis describes reading her *Tale of Squirrel Nutkin*. The book depicts, in words and unforgettable pictures, a mischievous squirrel gathering nuts. He taunts Old Owl sitting in the tree, who suddenly breaks out of his lethargy and grabs the squirrel, who barely escapes at the expense of his tail. Probably referring to the book's illustrations of leaves and trees in fall colors, Lewis writes that *Squirrel Nutkin* "troubled" him with "the Idea of Autumn." It made him "enamored of a season." "As before, the experience was one of intense desire."[6]

In reality, this story amounts to nothing more than a mere children's book, and yet for Lewis this experience contained the same surprise and sense of incalculable importance as his brother's imaginary garden. It was something quite different from ordinary life and even from ordinary pleasure; something, as they would now say, "in another dimension."[7] But this children's book mediated to young Lewis an experience of nature ("the Idea of Autumn") that was, at the same time, transcendent—even otherworldly.

Beatrix Potter is surely a major influence on the way Lewis portrayed his animals in The Chronicles of Narnia. Her talking hedgehogs, pigs, and rabbits—dressed, as the citizens of Boxen were, in little coats and dresses—were both humorous and tough minded. And in their adventures and in the illustrations that accompanied them—with their rural kitchens and cozy burrows—they embodied a quality Lewis loved: "homeliness." By that he meant "the rooted quality" attached "to all our simple experiences, to weather, food, the family, the neighborhood."[8] In *The Lion, the Witch and the Wardrobe*, Mr. and Mrs. Beaver, bustling about in their snug lodge, putting out wholesome meals, exemplify this homeliness; and it continues throughout The Chronicles of Narnia.

But the real charm of Beatrix Potter's characters is that while they speak, reason, and wear clothes like human beings, they are, at the same time, recognizably and essentially animals. Peter Rabbit may capture perfectly the personality of a disobedient child, but he is also a wild rabbit scampering through Mr. McGregor's garden patch. And C. S. Lewis's talking animals are like that. When Caspian meets the Bulgy Bears, they are slow and ponderous characters who snuffle him and offer him some honey. They are rational, but bearlike. Likewise, the squirrel Pattertwig demonstrates his "squirrelness" by bounding from branch to branch and constantly chattering.

These animal qualities combined with human characteristics often result in truly memorable characters. But more important, these characters represent for Lewis the personality, meaning, and loveableness that he finds in the natural order. With what pity, then, Lewis must have looked on the New Narnian world as it tried to reduce nature to an impersonal mechanism. Unfortunately, this is exactly what is happening in our own world—we seek not only to eliminate "God" from the natural order of things, but in many cases we seek to eliminate the notion of a natural order altogether.

AN UNNATURAL ORDER

Clearly Lewis is reacting against the modernist mind-set that seeks to remove the notion of God from the natural world. However, this mind-set can be difficult to discern, since at first glance it often appears to advocate nature's virtues. For when God is banished, as He has been from much of our world today, something must fill the void. So, many modernists try to fill that God-shaped void with nature. Now, nature is often worshipped as a "god" in its own right.

More specifically, the divinization of nature takes place when we ascribe to it God's attributes. "The cosmos," Carl Sagan said, "is all there is, there was, or ever will be."[9] Here he is echoing Revelation 1:8: "'I am the Alpha and the Omega,' says the Lord God, 'who is and who was and who is to come, the Almighty.'" Sagan simply replaces "the Lord God" with "the cosmos." According to this worldview, nature is eternal, infinite, uncreated, and omnipresent.

And yet, those who have built nature up are the same ones who diminish its importance. Animals, trees, water, planets are all seen as nothing more than collections of atoms that have randomly come together. According to Sagan, nature is infinite, yet this worldview seems immensely narrow. It hems in the human spirit to the point of claustrophobia. We become like Hamlet: "I could be bounded in a nut-shell, and count myself a king of infinite space, were it not that I have bad dreams."[10]

Meanwhile, we modernists take apart the natural order, ravage it, and bend it to our will. According to Lewis, we "cut down trees whenever we can" and are "at war with all wild things."[11] Lewis would surely agree with the Romantic poets in their critiques of industrialism and materialistic science. The scientific intellect analyzes nature to the point of killing it, says Wordsworth: "We murder to dissect."[12] Instead of living in a natural landscape, today we live in a world dominated and created by machines. Blake called the ugly, smoke-spewing factories blighting the countryside "dark

Satanic mills."[13]

Commercialism, the impulse to turn God's creation into a set of commodities to buy and sell, also cuts us off from nature. Hopkins complained, "All is seared with trade; / Bleared, smeared with toil, / And wears man's smudge and shares man's smell."[14]

In the New Narnia, the Telmarines have disenchanted nature. That is, they have taken away the sense of mystery, beauty, and spiritual significance that nature used to inspire. Animals have lost their speech. The trees have gone to sleep. "Since the Humans came into the land, felling forests and defiling streams," an Old Narnian complains, "the dryads [tree spirits] and naiads [water spirits] have sunk into a deep sleep."[15]

But Prince Caspian is forced to experience nature in a genuine way, and as he does so, he begins to transform from child to king. What he once feared as unknown soon became a part of him. "To sleep under the stars, to drink nothing but well water and to live chiefly on nuts and wild fruit, was a strange experience for Caspian." He was used to living in a castle, sleeping on silk sheets, and eating with a silver spoon while servants attended to his every desire. But now, living out of doors, and despite the relative hardship, "he had never enjoyed himself more." He slept better than ever. Food never tasted so good. His body hardened. "His face wore a kinglier look."[16]

THE NATURAL LAW

But it is not just nature in the sense of wildlife, mountains, and oceans that has become diminished in modern life. Indeed, people today may glorify these things while still denigrating natural law.

For Old Western thinkers, "nature" had a broader meaning than just plants and animals; it meant objective reality. That certainly included trees and wildlife, but, more importantly, it included the structure of physical reality, a "natural law" that both humans and societies are subject to.

Actually, the word "nature" originally referred to the qualities that make up the essence of something. This sense still survives in statements such as, "Hunting is part of a cat's nature." We also debate about "the nature of democracy" or "the nature of science" and speak of "human nature." The assumption behind this language is that cats have something that makes them cats, that democracy and science have characteristics that make them what they are, and that we have specific objective qualities that make us human.

What we said about Lewis's talking animals illustrates the point. While some of these Narnian beasts are rational and have language, they still exhibit their animal *natures*. Pattertwig still has his squirrel nature, leaping around and chattering. When Trufflehunter sinks his teeth into something, like all badgers, he does not let go.

Everything has its "nature," and everything is subject to "the laws of nature." Today when we hear the phrase "natural law," we think of physics and chemistry, the scientifically predictable properties of physical objects. But for classical thinkers, "natural law" also refers to moral reality. Today, the common assumption is that morality is cultural or a matter of individual preference. But in classical thought, morality has to do with objective truth, built into the very fabric of reality.

According to natural law theory, morality is not a set of arbitrary rules that can be changed or violated at will. To a great degree, morality is comprehensible to reason. Consider sexual morality. The biological purpose of sexuality is to engender children. Everything about sex, down to the tiniest physiological detail, is designed to create new life. This is why, for human beings, sexual activity is reserved for marriage, that family relationship designed to bring children into the world and care for them. Sex outside of marriage—recreational sex, homosexuality, indulgence in pornography—is literally "unnatural." That means it is the pursuit of sex apart from the nature of sex. (I am not saying that the *only* purpose of sex is engendering children, but this is its *biological* purpose—its *natural* design.)

Notice that, according to this worldview, nature and the elements of nature have "purpose." They are designed. This is in contrast to the modernist and postmodernist view that nature is random and purposeless, as Darwinists insist, and meaningless, as existentialists insist. Rather, nature is rational, which is evidence of a Mind that looms behind it. Nature is objectively ordered, which is evidence that points to its Creator. This way of thinking had its origins in Plato and Aristotle, but it was adopted by Christian thinkers such as Thomas Aquinas and the Reformers, who took the logical next step of relating the natural law to the law of God.

When C. S. Lewis begins *Mere Christianity* by arguing for the objective reality of the moral law—working with tangible examples such as someone taking your seat on a bus—he is making the case for natural law. He has to begin here in his Christian apologetic because his contemporary audience tends not to believe in morality any more than they believe in God. But Lewis the evangelist knows that the law must precede the gospel, that people must be convicted of their sin before they will awaken to their need for a Savior.

His book *The Abolition of Man* is a more scholarly defense of natural law. In it Lewis shows that moral judgments presuppose an objective order, which he calls the *Tao*, and that to reduce morality to mere subjective feelings, as is generally done today, leads to the abolition of human nature. He also cites evidence from various cultures and religions that demonstrates how basic moral teachings are in fact not cultural constructions at all, but rather universal laws.

In *Prince Caspian*, the Telmarines have vandalized not only the natural landscape, but also the natural law, as is represented most profoundly by King Miraz. He killed his own brother, violating nature's fundamental unit, the family. He crowned himself king when he had no natural right to the throne, violating the state, an institution necessary for human nature. He even attempted to kill his own nephew, Caspian, who was just a child, whereas adults by nature are supposed to protect children. Caspian was violating not only the societal laws of his country but also the universal laws of the human race.

When the Pevensies finally make their way to Aslan's How and join the Old Narnians, Peter dictates a document to Dr. Cornelius that will indict Miraz and challenge him to single combat. The charge against him, which Peter insists be written in the archaic style of Old Narnia, is that Miraz is "*twice guilty of treachery both in withholding the dominion of Narnia from the said Caspian and in the most abhominable*—don't forget to spell it with an H, Doctor—*bloody, and unnatural murder of your kindly lord and brother King Caspian Ninth of that name.*"[17]

Miraz and everything he stands for are "unnatural."

THE GREAT CHAIN OF BEING

Another important dimension of nature, as it was known in Old Western civilization, is the ordered hierarchy of all creation. Lewis alludes to this on the night Lucy meets Aslan in the woods as the others were sleeping. As Lucy made her way through the darkness, she noticed that the trees were dancing, and she could sense all of a sudden that she was part of a "Great Chain."[18] This alludes to what classical thinkers called the "Great Chain of Being."

Evolutionists note the gradations of life from the simple to the more complex, from single-celled microorganisms to colonies of cells such as sponges, then to creatures with differentiated organs: worms, fish, reptiles, mammals, etc. Darwinists assume that these different species turned into each other, even though they each exist separately today. The Old Western scientists saw the same data, but to them it was evidence of a great order, in which every part of the creation had its place in the hierarchies of existence.

Within each category, each kind has its place in the chain. Even inanimate objects, such as stones and metals, exist in hierarchies, similar to the periodic table of modern chemistry. Plants had their hierarchies, from moss to grass to trees. And so did animals, in a sense that lions really could be thought of as the king of beasts. And human beings have their hierarchies and natural authorities as well, which to the ancient mind blurred the boundaries between nature and society. Above children were their parents, above woman was man, above commoners were the nobility, and above nobility was royalty.

Yes, those human hierarchies grate on us now, but the worldview of the Great Chain of Being—which Lewis explores in *The Discarded Image*—is where they came from. Still, someone whose worldview included a belief in the Great Chain of Being would see himself or herself as occupying a distinct niche in the universe. Everything has its place. This model of the universe gave its inhabitants something that people today almost never feel: the security of feeling at home in the universe, not alienated, but of living in a world of meaning and order.

They perhaps needed to take into greater account the radical magnitude of the fall, which threw disorder into nature and which gave human beings the lust to dominate and oppress each other. But still, according to the ancient cosmology, what tied the universe together and put it into motion was love. As Dante unforgettably portrays in the conclusion of his *Divine Comedy*, it is love—the attraction not only of people for each other, but of objects for each other and of God for His creation—that moves the sun and the stars.[19]

Thus, cruelty and tyranny are also unnatural. One difference between animal nature and human nature, according to the Old Western thinkers, is that human nature includes freedom. Human beings can therefore be "unnatural" in a way that animals and plants cannot in that they can deprive each other of freedom.

At any rate, *Prince Caspian* includes a distinctly biblical take on the Great Chain of Being. When the Old Narnians find Caspian, the dwarf Nikabrik first wants to kill him. But when they learn his identity, the badger Trufflehunter says that he is "a true king, come back to true Narnia."[20] Narnia is only right, he says, when a Son of Adam is king.

Nikabrik cannot believe his ears. The badger wants to give over the whole country to humans—to a Telmarine, no less. But, says Trufflehunter, that is not the point. "It's not Men's country," he says. "But it's a country for a man to be King of."[21]

Caspian is a Son of Adam. Trufflehunter knows that even in Narnia Adam and his descendents were given sovereignty over animals:

> Then God said, "Let us make man in our image, after our likeness. And let them have dominion over the fish of the sea and over the birds of the heavens and over the livestock and over all the earth and over every creeping thing that creeps on the earth." (Gen. 1:26)

Later, we learn that the Telmarines descended from pirates, who transported from Earth to Narnia in much the same way the Pevensies did. When Aslan tells Caspian of his pirate ancestry, the young king is ashamed of his low lineage. Aslan says, "You come of the Lord Adam and the Lady Eve.... That is both honor enough to erect the head of the poorest beggar, and shame enough to bow the shoulders of the greatest emperor in earth."[22]

Any human—including the four middle-class Pevensies—is

royalty in Narnia. Not by virtue of a social hierarchy but because of the dominion they inherited from Adam and Eve. That is, because of their human nature.

In *The Abolition of Man*, Lewis worries that our rejection of the natural moral law will lead eventually to the undoing of our human nature. This is the danger he sees, both in the "New West" and in the New Narnia.

At one point in the course of their travels, the Pevensies are attacked by a bear. It is not a talking bear, just a wild and dangerous animal, which is what many of the animals have degenerated into during the long Telmarine reign. They kill the bear, and Lucy wonders, "Wouldn't it be dreadful if some day in our own world, at home, men started going wild inside, like the animals here, and still looked like men, so that you'd never know which were which?"[23]

When human beings act like animals—when they are brutal, when they refuse to control their passions, when they prey on others—they are not being "natural." As is often said, they are imitating the promiscuity and predations of lesser animals. Animal-like humans are literally "unnatural," rejecting the rationality and conscience that are part of human nature.

The animals in Narnia once had the gift of speech and reason, but over 1,288 years they have lost those higher faculties and gone wild. Lewis's fear is that something similar could happen in our world as we get used to being "unnatural." In truth, something similar to that already has happened and has been happening for some time. In *The Abolition of Man*, Lewis related the rejection of natural law to the rise of tyranny in the twentieth

century. It is no great stretch to draw parallels between such dic-
tators as Hitler and Stalin and the evil King Miraz. But if we do
not act quickly to recover the lost hierarchies of our human
nature—such as the natural law that parents should nourish their
children rather than abort or abandon them, that knowledge
should serve humanity rather than destroy or engineer it, that
passions must be self-controlled rather than unleashed—then
these will not be the last examples that our world will ever see of
"men ... going wild inside."

STUDY QUESTIONS

1. Have you ever experienced a feeling of "transcendence" or "enormous bliss," like Lewis did beneath the flowering currant bush? If so, where or when? If not, why do you think that is?

2. When was the last time you completely submerged yourself in nature and considered the beauty of God's created order? What can you do to ensure such experiences occur more frequently?

3. Lewis seems to lament the loss of the mystery, beauty, and spiritual significance of nature in Narnia. An Old Narnian voiced his complaint, "Since the Humans came into the land, felling forests and defiling streams, the dryads and naiads have sunk into a deep sleep."

In what way does this observation reflect what has happened in our own world?

4. At one point, Aslan says, "You come of the Lord Adam and the Lady Eve.... That is both honor enough to erect the head of the poorest beggar, and shame enough to bow the shoulders of the greatest emperor in earth."

What do you think of this statement? Do you feel like you carry more honor or shame? Why? How can we claim the royalty of our heritage?

5. Think about Lucy's question: "Wouldn't it be dreadful if some day in our own world, at home, men started going wild inside, like the animals here, so that you'd never know which were

which?" How is this already occurring in our own world? What does that mean for us as Christians?

$\mathscr{Seven}$
MYTH: NOT SAFE WITHOUT ASLAN

"I wouldn't have felt very safe with Bacchus and
all his wild girls if we'd met them without Aslan."
"I should think not."

—Susan and Lucy, chapter 11

Some Christians are bothered with C. S. Lewis's practice of bringing elements from pagan mythology into Narnia. Even the faun in
The Lion, the Witch and the Wardrobe is too much for some readers, though most are able to get past it. But *Prince Caspian* goes
much further in incorporating pagan myth into an otherwise
Christian tale.

When Aslan comes on the scene, he roars, and all Narnia
awakens. The forests come alive as the trees all join in the dance.
Animals pop out of their lairs. What the ancient Greeks recog-
nized as local nature spirits—nymphs, naiads, dryads, even a
river god—come out of their deep slumber.

But then comes someone who exemplifies not the great ideas

of the ancient Greeks, but rather their pagan religion: a wild boy, clad only in a fawn skin, his hair wreathed with vine leaves, dancing and frolicking. With him are a company of wild girls and a fat man on a donkey. Wherever they go, vines laden with grapes spring up. They laugh and call out a mysterious cry, "Euan, euan, eu-oi-oi-oi!"[1]

In ancient Greek and Rome, this was the cry of the Bacchantes, the frenzied worshippers of Bacchus, the god of wine. "Bacchus" was just one of the many names for Dionysus, patron of wine and fertility who was associated with ecstasy and even madness. The fat man on the donkey is Silenus, Bacchus's comical but supposedly wise old teacher.

In a sort of odd twist on tradition, though, in *Prince Caspian* Bacchus and his crew are followers of Aslan. Even further, they play an important role in the subsequent liberation of Narnia, which we will discuss in chapter 10. But for now, we must ask the question, how and why could Lewis combine pagan myth with Christian truth?

THE BIBLICAL AND THE CLASSICAL

J. R. R. Tolkien disapproved of the Narnia books for several reasons, one of which was because of the way his friend Lewis combined different mythologies. Narnia is populated with nature deities from Greek mythology, dwarfs and giants from Germanic mythology, and knights and quests from medieval legends, among others. To top it off, we even get an appearance in *The Lion, the Witch and the Wardrobe* of Father Christmas, whom most of us know as Santa Claus! Tolkien did not object to this mythological melting pot on any kind of theological grounds, but simply because he was a mythological purist. (Tolkien's other objection was that Lewis was mixing fantasy with the real world, with characters moving back and forth from one realm to the other. Tolkien believed fantasy subcreations should be consistent, self-contained, and set apart, as he achieved in Middle-earth.)[2]

And yet, Lewis was in good company with his weaving of myth. One of the greatest English poets, Edmund Spenser, did something very similar in *The Faerie Queene*. In his day job at Oxford and Cambridge, Lewis was, among his other areas of expertise, a noted Spenser scholar.[3] Much like Lewis's Narnia, Spenser's Faerie Land was also a fantasy world inhabited by denizens from classical myth, medieval romance, and English folklore. In Spenser's tales, a young prince, who would later become King Arthur, travels between medieval England and the strange world of Faerie Land. But most importantly, Spenser's fantasy is also an allegory of Christianity, combining enjoyable story for its own sake with passages of intense symbolism that explore the Christian faith and the Reformation emphasis on grace, faith, and the Bible.

The very structure of each Narnia book points back to *The Faerie Queene* as a model. It was Lewis himself who first pointed out that each of the six books of *The Faerie Queene* contains a specific allegorical episode that symbolizes the particular theme of that book.[4] Lewis carried that scholarly observation into his own fiction when he wrote The Chronicles of Narnia, in which each book contains a similar symbolic core involving Aslan. In *The Lion, the Witch and the Wardrobe*, the main theme is the sacrifice and resurrection of Aslan, while *Prince Caspian* portrays the "divine revel," which we will discuss in chapter 10. (Once you get the idea, you can easily find the key symbolic scene in the other books.)

But as for mixing Christianity with figures from ancient Greek mythology, neither Lewis nor Spenser is alone. Milton, Lewis's other favorite literary specialty, included ancient mythology in his works as well. As did Dante. In fact, nearly all the classical thinkers of Old Europe could be counted in this group, including the visual artists of the Renaissance and Reformation.

Before modernist progressive education became popular, classical education was the preferred method. The classical approach to education, which a number of Christian schools and homeschools are working to bring back, has many dimensions,[5] but for Lewis and nearly all educated people before him, it included mastery of the languages and literature of ancient Greece and Rome.[6]

The early church, made up largely of Greeks and Romans and those who spoke their languages, did not completely repudiate their heritage. The church rejected the pagan religious beliefs but kept the stories. Once people understood the myths to be untrue, they accepted them as works of fiction. And their admirers saw in the myths, as they saw in other works of fiction, themes that were highly relevant to human life and that were consistent with the Christian faith.[7] Athena, the goddess of wisdom, did not really take the human form of an old man named Mentor and give advice to young heroes. But that story, purged of Athena worship, has thematic truth: Young people can benefit from wise and experienced counselors, thus giving us the noun and the verb "mentor."

Christians read *The Odyssey*, in which Odysseus must resist the song of the Sirens, the opiate of the Lotus Eaters, and the seductions of Calypso in order to reach his true home, as a profound treatise on the need to resist temptation. Even the myth of Dionysus, as we shall see, contains certain ideas that are relevant to the Christian faith.

THE ANCIENT AND THE MODERN

Another factor in C. S. Lewis's use of Greek mythology in *Prince Caspian* is his belief that, when it comes to the new worldviews that characterize the modern world, Christians and the ancient pagans are on the same side. "Christians and Pagans had much more in common with each other than either has with a post-Christian," Lewis said in the Cambridge address discussed in chapter 3. "The gap between those who worship different gods is not so wide as that between those who worship and those who do not."[8]

Lewis rejects the view that the modern world is reverting back to paganism. "It might be rather fun if we were," he said, recalling a point G. K. Chesterton once made. "It would be pleasant to see some future Prime Minister trying to kill a large and lively milk-white bull in Westminster Hall."[9] Rather, what Lewis is most concerned with, both in that address and in *Prince Caspian*, is what he calls the "un-christening" of Western culture:

> The christening of Europe seemed to all our
> ancestors, whether they welcomed it themselves
> as Christians, or, like Gibbon, deplored it as

humanistic unbelievers, a unique, irreversible event. But we have seen the opposite process. Of course the un-christening of Europe in our time is not quite complete; neither was her christening in the Dark Ages. But roughly speaking we may say that whereas all history was for our ancestors divided into two periods, the pre-Christian and the Christian, and two only, for us it falls into three—the pre-Christian, the Christian, and what may reasonably be called the post-Christian.... It appears to me that the second change is even more radical than the first.... Of course there were lots of skeptics in Jane Austen's time and long before, as there are lots of Christians now. But the presumption has changed. In her day some kind and degree of religious belief and practice were the norm; now, though I would gladly believe that both kind and degree have improved, they are the exception.[10]

The pre-Christian and the Christian did more than agree on the existence of deities. The controversy today is not just over whether God exists. Now that modernism has given way to postmodernism, the controversy is over whether *nature* exists. The conventional wisdom today is that nothing has a "nature," an objective essence. Under this pretense, nature itself, as the realm of objective reality, evaporates. Postmodernists believe that what we think of as reality is nothing more than a cultural or personal construction. Truth, at worst, is an imposition of power, a construction designed to keep certain people in power and oppress the rest. Truth, at best, is relative. We all have our own truths, and no one person's truth is any more valid than anyone else's.

To classical thinkers, such as Plato and Aristotle, the objective realm does exist. It is not elusive but knowable, not random but orderly, not meaningless but rational. Plato and Aristotle were the foundational analysts of the "natural law" that we discussed in the last chapter. They saw the connection between nature, human nature, and the moral law. Truth exists; morality is objective and related to that truth. And underlying not only truth but existence itself, according to the profoundest Greek philosophers, is the *logos*, a rational structure they called "the word." The apostle John identified this classical concept with Jesus Christ, teaching that "in the beginning was the *logos*":

> In the beginning was the Word, and the Word was with God, and the Word was God. He was in the beginning with God. All things were made through him, and without him was not any thing made that was made. In him was life, and the life was the light of men.... And the Word became flesh and dwelt among us, and we have seen his glory, glory as of the only Son from the Father, full of grace and truth. (John 1:1–4, 14)

The point is, on the level of worldview, Christianity has always found itself compatible with classical thought. Not that they were identical, because sometimes they were in conflict. But they were at least playing on the same field.

From the days of ancient Rome through the eighteenth century—and in some places, such as Lewis's schools and universities, into the twentieth century—classical thought and literature dominated the educational curriculum. This classical heritage from Greece and Rome, combined with the biblical heritage of Jews and Christians, gave us what Lewis called "Old Western" civilization, which the "New West" (like New Narnia) has now rejected.

MYTH

Lewis loved myth. Not the "irreverent, silly myths" Paul warned against in 1 Timothy 4:7, but ancient stories that stirred his imagination and gave him a taste of transcendent joy and desire. In fact, myth was instrumental in eventually leading him to faith. In *Surprised by Joy*, Lewis tells how in childhood and even on into adulthood he would pore over mythological tales (such as those of the ancient Norse) and newer works (such as Wagner's operas and George MacDonald's adult fairy tale, *Phantastes*). Such stories stirred in him deep longings, which he described as "joy."

Lewis carried on his fascination with such tales as a literary scholar and then later as a fantasy writer. In 1929, when Lewis was thirty-two years old, after a long intellectual and personal struggle, he finally relented and allowed himself to believe in God. In his words, "I gave in, and admitted that God was God, and knelt and prayed: perhaps, that night, the most dejected and reluctant convert in all England."[11]

He was not necessarily a Christian yet, as he had not accepted the gospel of Christ, but it would not take long for him to make the connection—three short years, in fact. As Lewis biographer George Sayer describes it, Lewis and his good friend J. R. R. Tolkien, along with another Christian named Hugo Dyson, went for a walk one night after dinner.[12] They were talking about myth when Lewis said that he loved myths, even though they were not true. Tolkien challenged this assumption. Myths, Tolkien said, have their origin in God. They contain some remnants of God's truth, though that truth is distorted. Many cultures have myths of a dying god who gives his life for his people, and these myths are but a shadow of a real truth—that Jesus Christ really did die and rise again. Not in the vague sense of "once upon a time," but in actual history. Christianity is not mythological but historical. As Lewis later put it, in Christianity "myth became fact."[13] Tolkien pressed him further: If you respond to myth, he pointed out, you should also respond to Christ. "Tolkien went on to explain," summarized Sayer, "that the Christian story was a myth invented by a God who was real, a God whose dying could transform those who believed in him."[14]

They kept talking until three o'clock in the morning. According to Sayer, after Tolkien went home "Dyson and Lewis continued talking, striding up and down the arcades of New Buildings [at Oxford's Magdalene College]. Dyson's main point was that Christianity works for the believer. The believer is put at peace and freed from his sins. He receives help in overcoming his faults and can become a new person."[15] Two days later, Lewis recorded, "I was driven to Whipsnade one sunny morning. When we set out I did not believe that Jesus Christ is the Son of God, and when we reached the zoo I did."[16] Lewis later expanded on the sense in which, in Christ, myth became fact:

> Now as myth transcends thought, Incarnation transcends myth. The heart of Christianity is a myth which is also a fact. The old myth of the Dying God, *without ceasing to be myth* comes down from the heaven of legend and imagination to the earth of history. It *happens*—at a particular date, in a particular place, followed by definable historical consequences. We pass from a Balder or an Osiris, dying nobody knows when or where, to a historical Person crucified (it is all in order) *under Pontius Pilate*. By becoming fact it does not cease to be myth: that is the miracle.[17]

"Christians also need to be reminded," Lewis added, "that what became Fact was a Myth, that it carries with it into the world of Fact all the properties of a myth. God is more than a god, not less; Christ is more than Balder, not less. We must not be ashamed of the mythical radiance resting on our theology."[18]

And one of these dying gods, according to Greek mythology, was Dionysus. When the wild Bacchus of *Prince Caspian* was a baby, evil Titans supposedly lured him with toys, then tore him apart and ate him. But his father, Zeus, the king of the gods, found his heart and brought him back to life.[19]

To Lewis, at least, Dionysus and other dying gods of mythology point to Christ. He did not believe in *them* per se. They are myths, and, in their own terms, deities of false religions. But taken as fiction, like other works of fiction, they have a meaning—they point to something. That meaning ultimately can be traced back to the divine *logos* that underlies all creation.

THE DIONYSIAN AND THE APOLLONIAN

But Lewis is doing something else when he brings in Bacchus to cavort with Aslan. Myth can also be a way to encapsulate ideas. One of the most notable uses of myth on the part of scholars to capture different categories of experience is the contrast between Apollo and Dionysus and the impulses they represent.

Apollo is the god of order, rationality, and objectivity. He is the sun god and so represents light and illumination. Dionysus is the god of disorder, passion, and subjectivity. He is the god of wine and so represents wildness and ecstasy.

This dichotomy represents the polar opposites of human experience and creativity. The classical style, with its external forms, idealized art, and lucid poetry, is Apollonian. The Romantic style, with its organic forms, emotional art, and inward poetry, is Dionysian. Some cultures are Apollonian, oriented to law and order, self-restraint, and sober-mindedness. Other cultures are Dionysian, favoring freedom, wildness, and emotional expression.

Applying these categories was popular in scholarly circles during Lewis's day. The pioneering American anthropologist Ruth Benedict, for example, showed how the Pueblo Indians of the Southwest were Apollonian, with their stable adobe dwellings, their value of self-control, and their calm and restrained rituals. The American Indians of the Great Plains, on the other hand, such as the Comanche and the Sioux, were Dionysian: They lived in mobile tents, gave in to their impulses, and worshipped by going into a frenzy.[20]

Lewis alludes to these "Dionysian" qualities with the depiction of Bacchus in *Prince Caspian*. His face was "extremely wild," and the girls who accompanied him were "as wild as he." And Bacchus was dangerous. He seemed to acknowledge no limits. "There is a chap who might do anything," observed Edmund. "Absolutely anything."[21]

But here Bacchus and his revelers are dancing around Aslan. Their faces are turned toward the great beast, "to hear what he would say next."[22] This Dionysus, uncharacteristically, is symbolically celebrating Christ by listening to His Word. He is under God's control, while still embodying ecstatic freedom.

Lewis saw Christianity as not just one religion among many, but as embracing and fulfilling the whole range of spiritual truth and experience. All other religions—and myths—are partial and incomplete. Christianity is both Apollonian *and* Dionysian. It has both doctrines and experiences, law and liberation, systematic theologies and bloody sacrifices. In Lewis's terms, Christianity is both "thick" and "clear." He explained:

> By *Thick*, I mean those which have orgies and ecstasies and mysteries and local attachments: Africa is full of Thick religions. By *Clear*, I mean those which are philosophical, ethical and universalizing: Stoicism, Buddhism, and the Ethical Church are Clear religions.

Now if there is a true religion it must be both
Thick and Clear: for the true God must have
made both the child and the man, both the savage and the citizen, both the head and the
belly.... Christianity ... takes a convert from central Africa and tells him to obey an enlightened
universalist ethic; it takes a twentieth-century
academic prig like me and tells me to go fasting
to a Mystery, to drink the blood of the Lord. The
savage convert has to be Clear. I have to be Thick.
That is how one knows one has come to the real
religion.[23]

Lewis sees the necessity of balance: A rationalist needs to cultivate his emotions. Someone who is emotional needs to learn how
to think rationally. Christianity, unlike other religions, which are
one thing or the other, is complete.

Again, as we discussed in chapter 4, Lewis, the self-described
defender of Reason, Romanticism, and Christianity, is countering
what T. S. Eliot called "the dissociation of sensibility." Modernism,
that ideology of scientific materialism born in "the Age of Reason,"
is Apollonian. Postmodernism, in contrast, is Dionysian. But here
in *Prince Caspian*, Lewis is primarily concerned with the atheism,
reductionism, and controlling tyranny of the New Narnians. The
Telmarines and skeptical dwarfs need to be freed from their mech-
anistic ideologies, and so Aslan frees them through the wild
example of Bacchus. He shows them what it really means to live
with the excitement of the Lord.

Be careful, though, for this by no means is an endorsement of the Dionysian impulse in itself, apart from Christ. "I wouldn't have felt very safe with Bacchus and all his wild girls if we'd met them without Aslan," Susan said, underscoring the point that paganism, myth, and Dionysian experience are dangerous on their own.[24] Without Christ, they are idolatrous and destructive.

Thus, Lewis is *not* being pagan when he brings into his story characters from pagan myth. Rather, he is showing how pagan deities can point to Christ. When Christ is the center, with myths literally dancing around Him, the classical realm gains a new and powerful significance. Indeed, when allowed to operate as it is designed—to illuminate some deeper truth of creation hidden within the human soul—myth can become a powerful tool for the gospel of Christ.

STUDY QUESTIONS

1. What do you think of the "wildness" of Bacchus in the story? Are there any biblical characters he reminds you of? Why? Which aspects of his character do you wish you could emulate more in your own faith?

2. What do you think of the "un-christening" of our culture? Do you agree with Lewis that this is even worse than reverting back to a pagan culture? How does your local church address this issue? How do you think it should?

3. What do you think of the idea that truth is relative? That something may be true for you, but not for someone else? How can you address this notion in your own faith and in how you relate to others?

4. How did you come to faith in Christ? Was it a struggle, like for Lewis? Why or why not?

5. Would you consider yourself more Dionysian or Apollonian? How do these qualities reveal themselves in you? Why is it important for a Christian to have a little of both?

6. How can one be under God's control and still embody ecstatic freedom? Would you describe yourself as being ecstatically free? What or why not? If not, how can you grow that side of yourself?

Eight
TEMPTATIONS: HOW CULTURE WARRIORS LOSE

"We want power: and we want power that will be on our side. As for power, do not the stories say that the Witch defeated Aslan, and bound him, and killed him on that very stone which is over there, just beyond the light? ... What came of the Kings and their reign? They faded too. But it's very different with the Witch. They say she ruled for a hundred years: a hundred years of winter. There's power, if you like. There's something practical."
—Nikabrik to the Old Narnian council, chapter 12

C. S. Lewis, like most Christian writers through the centuries, had no problem drawing on classical mythology. But he by no means embraced any kind of pagan or occult spirituality. In fact, a major theme of *Prince Caspian* has to do with the danger of the occult and other temptations that can sidetrack us from our commendable goals.

Late in the story, when the Old Narnians realize they may be fighting a losing battle, some declare their desire to call on an even older power than the kings and queens of old—they wish to call on the White Witch and everything she stands for. This of course would amount not only to a spiritual alliance with the Devil, but also to an endorsement of what he represents, which includes the rejection of moral restraints, the pursuit of power at any cost, and the belief that the ends justify the means.

As the old saying goes: "Power corrupts. Absolute power corrupts absolutely." Those who desire positive change often allow themselves to turn into the very thing they seek to overthrow. Oppressed Frenchmen in the eighteenth century staged a revolution for the rights of man, and then executed those rights at the guillotine. Separatist guerrillas start as freedom fighters but then form new dictatorships. Conservative activists lobby for smaller government only to build larger governments that further their own agendas. Moral crusaders often act immorally in their fund-raising and in how they treat their staff and families. I could go on.

This is not to say that all those who seek change will fall victim to such temptations. But there are pitfalls along the way for those who do not have the purest intentions *always* in their minds. "Restoring the true religion" is not just a matter of winning battles and seizing political power. The ends do *not* justify the means, and those who wish to affect their culture in a positive manner must abide by certain spiritual and moral requirements. In *Prince Caspian*, Lewis shows how those who wish to join the fight—whether in Narnia or our world—may face temptations of illicit power, which they must resist at any cost.

Other Powers in Narnia

As mentioned earlier, just as the Old Narnians were reaching their time of greatest need, some of them were beginning to despair. They had just used Queen Susan's horn in an attempt to summon help, as the old stories told it would bring, but to their knowledge nothing had happened. No help was coming. They began to wonder, what if the legends weren't true? Or worse yet, what if Aslan was not on their side? According to the old stories, he was not always a friend to dwarfs. Nor to some of the other talking animals, such as the wolves.

Seeing no other option, some of the less-faithful dwarfs, chiefly Nikabrik, decide to seek help elsewhere. He summons to their high council two guests whom no one had ever seen before: an old woman and a hooded man.

With an ingratiating tone, the old woman soon reveals her purpose—that she has some experience casting spells and, with permission, would gladly use them against the Telmarines. She hates them, she says. And no one can hate as well as she can, for she is a hag, or a witch—the personification of hate itself. Activists in a good cause are often tempted to hate their opponents, giving in to an emotion that can twist their souls and poison their principles. But clearly, indulging in hatred can put one in dangerous company.

Similarly, the dwarf's other guest—the hooded man—soon reveals his intentions as well. He calls himself hunger and thirst and says that when he bites, he never lets go—even in death his grip remains strong. He claims he can drink a river of blood and asks to be set loose on the enemy. He is a werewolf, the very symbol of cruelty. His brand of ruthlessness results in absolute power, but at the expense of all goodness and decency.

Though the notion of such measures seems abhorrent, the cultivation of these sentiments is precisely what can turn pious idealists into terrorists. God never indulges sin, not even in a good cause, but certain spiritual powers begin to seem more appealing to us when options run low. In Nikabrik's case, he is led to believe that a power greater than that of Aslan controlled all of Narnia in the distant past. In fact, this power was so much greater than Aslan that it killed him. Nikabrik's response to the oppressions of the Telmarines and their materialistic worldview, therefore, is to go back before the redemption wrought by Aslan, to an even Older Narnia, where it was always winter but never Christmas. Nikabrik wants to bring back the White Witch.

Lewis includes an important warning here for Christians. Notice that the conflict in Narnia is not simply between the religious and the secular. In Narnia, as in our world, we see people with different beliefs and motives who have come together against a common opponent. The Old Narnians include both religious believers, such as Trufflehunter, and skeptics who are nevertheless traditionalists, such as Trumpkin and Nikabrik. Christian activists often ally themselves with political conservatives of various stripes who sometimes are not Christian at all.

Nothing is wrong, as such, with coalitions and tactical alliances. They are necessary in the political order. But Christian activists sometimes confuse the culture war with political war.

Culture has to do with morality; politics has to do with power. The two realms are related, and they can work hand in hand, but temptations arise when we become too focused on the latter.

Nikabrik's rejection of Aslan and subsequent acceptance of the White Witch is emblematic of three temptations that apply just as well in our world as they do in Narnia. For Nikabrik, as well as other Narnians I'm sure, these included a spiritual temptation, a moral temptation, and a tactical temptation. Specifically, these were the allure of occult spirituality, the lust for power, and the appeal to pragmatism.

THE TEMPTATION OF THE OCCULT

Many modernists thought that religion would die out in the twentieth century, that the authority of science and the worldview of materialism would take its place. As they were with many other things, the modernists were wrong. The postmodernists of the twenty-first century, for the most part having rejected reason altogether, are quite open to the supernatural realm in all of its manifestations. Christianity, or at least the notion of a God who knows each of us personally and who cares for our well-being, is thus quite culturally relevant today.

The problem with postmodernists, however, is that, because they have rejected reason, they are open to almost any form of religion or supernatural manifestation and that they have few resources to distinguish between what is true and what is false. Furthermore, many want to believe in *all* religions at the same time, a view that accords much better with ancient polytheism than historic Christianity.

134 THE SOUL OF PRINCE CASPIAN

The postmodernist receptiveness to the supernatural is a genuine opening for Christianity, but after centuries of trying to accommodate modernism, Christians have worked hard to make the case for their faith in rational terms. This simply won't work for today's generations, which are reacting against rationalism. They *like* mystery—things don't always have to make perfect sense—and they often find Christianity, with its seemingly restrictive doctrines and cut-and-dry churches, unappealing. Christianity, as Lewis said, is both "clear" and "thick," but unfortunately, the "clear" is what comes through these days, and that simply doesn't appeal to everyone anymore.

So, many postmodernists, in their search for mystery and what they do not understand, get their satisfaction from Eastern mysticism, New Age spirituality, and the occult. In fact, we may even be seeing the rise of a new religion, which is rushing in to fill the secularist void. It has to do with "spirituality," not doctrines or institutions. It draws freely from all religions and is permissive rather than demanding. Some observers call it "Open Source Religion,"[1] and in a way it hearkens back to pre-Christian polytheism. It is also reminiscent of the syncretism condemned by the prophets, wherein ancient Hebrews presumed to combine worship of the true God with the worship of false gods from neighboring cultures, going so far as to set up idols inside God's temple.

If one wanted an alternative to modernism, it would make sense to go back to premodern times. Some who do this eventually discover historical Christianity and are satisfied. But others go *way* back, even before the beginnings of classical philosophy—which generally opposed the irrational side of paganism—to the "thick" paganism of spells, magic, and witchcraft. Thus we have the new vogue of Wicca, which is the ancient worship of natural forces, satanism, reincarnation, and so on. Thankfully, we are not quite there yet, as Lewis says, for we are not sacrificing bulls in the public square. But notice how fascinated our popular culture is with vampires, horror films, and sadistic violence. These "thick" religious beliefs of the past have very clearly earned a new foothold in today's world.

But perhaps what is even more common today, and more dangerous, are New Age beliefs, with their dogma of positive thinking, meditation techniques, and faith in the inner self. Some even adhere to such things as "pyramid power" or flying saucer worship. Such beliefs might seem silly when you really think about them, but for most people nowadays reason does not enter into the equation. For example, astrology is predicated upon the notion that the earth is the center of the universe, but this errant fact does not prevent millions of people from seeking guidance from their horoscopes in the daily newspapers. What such belief systems offer, then, is a domesticated spirituality—one can experience all the comforts of a mystical view of life without the "difficulties" of traditional religions, such as self-denial and repentance.

Lewis was mostly writing in a time of modernism, but the allure of the occult was already taking hold even in the early twentieth century. Lewis himself confessed to feeling it, to being tempted by it. In *Surprised by Joy*, he tells about how, at age thirteen, he attended a boarding school whose matron, a favorite teacher, was "floundering in the mazes of Theosophy,

Rosicrucianism, Spiritualism; the whole Anglo-American Occultist tradition." He said:

> I had never heard of such things before; never, except in a nightmare or a fairy tale, conceived of spirits other than God and men. I had loved to read of strange sights and other worlds and unknown modes of being, but never with the slightest belief.

> But now, for the first time, there burst upon me the idea that there might be real marvels all about us, that the visible world might be only a curtain to conceal huge realms unchartered by my very simple theology. And that started in me something with which, on and off, I have had plenty of trouble since—the desire for the preternatural, simply as such, the passion for the Occult.[2]

Lewis is harsh in denouncing this desire that he struggled with. He describes this passion for the occult as a "disease."[3] "It is a spiritual lust; and like the lust of the body it has the fatal power of making everything else in the world seem uninteresting while it lasts."[4]

The influence of the occult, Lewis said, while he was a teenager at this school, was a major factor in his giving up the Christian faith of his childhood. He did not blame his teacher; he blamed the Devil. "The Enemy did this in me, taking occasion from the things she innocently said. One reason why the Enemy found this so easy was that, without knowing it, I was already desperately anxious to get rid of my religion."[5]

Occultism carries with it a particular approach to spiritual issues, which goes beyond specific beliefs. What eroded away Lewis's Christianity was not some dark and evil experience, but a way of thinking about spiritual reality:

> The vagueness, the merely speculative character, of all this Occultism began to spread—yes, and to spread deliciously—to the stern truths of the creed. The whole thing became a matter of speculation: I was soon (in the famous words) altering "I believe" to "one does feel." And oh, the relief of it! ... From the tyrannous noon of revelation I passed into the cool evening of Higher Thought, where there was nothing to be obeyed, and nothing to be believed except what was either comforting or exciting.[6]

Does this sound familiar? Not only does this mind-set form the foundation for New Age beliefs and "Open Source Religion," but these same tendencies are present in contemporary Christianity. Much of our theology today is vague and speculative, unmoored from the revelation of God's Word. Many Christians are dismissive of doctrines and concerned only with how God makes them feel. We have watered down the Bible's morality as if there is "nothing to be obeyed," and the focus on much Christian teaching today is upon what is "comforting or exciting."

This is exactly the kind of pre-Aslanic approach to spiritual power Nikabrik is advocating. Occultism teaches us that we can disregard the authority of God's Word to plunge into the darkness that lies deep within the self. *We* are what's most important—not God. But because we are fallen and sinful, our innermost feelings are incapable of guiding us on their own. The inherent selfishness of our human nature will eventually take over, and we will be left with little more than the empty spirituality of the hag and the werewolf. Nikabrik was willing to believe in Aslan, if that would have helped rid Narnia of the Telmarines. He said, "I'll believe in anyone or anything ... that'll batter these cursed Telmarine barbarians to pieces or drive them out of Narnia. Anyone or anything, Aslan *or* the White Witch, do you understand?"[7]

And this is precisely why occultist beliefs are so dangerous: The desires of humanity are elevated while the sovereign will of God is subordinated. In this model, God is transformed from all-powerful Creator and Judge of heaven and Earth into a genie in a bottle. Such a god may be placated or appeased, conjured or manipulated, as long as personal fulfillment is achieved.

Unfortunately, again we hear echoes of some contemporary strains of Christianity. Many churches now preach the gospel of health and wealth, as opposed to the gospel of Christ. Follow certain principles, congregations are told, and you will have worldly success. According to one sermon I heard on television, if you want a new car, have faith that God will give it to you, and if you believe strongly enough, you will get it.

The "faith" this preacher was calling for was nothing more than a religiously dolled-up version of postmodern constructionism—the idea that each person creates his or her own reality. Whatever happened to "seek first the kingdom of God" (Matt. 6:33)? Or the notion that the "first will be last, and the last first" (Matt. 19:30)? These timeless truths have now been replaced by the "power of positive thinking." God is someone to be used for our own ends, which is how pagan religions use their deities. This theology, in effect, transforms Christianity into a pagan, occult religion.

Christians today often assume that to evangelize the world they must change their teaching and practices—they must think like the world to be more appealing to the world. But with this tactic, who is evangelizing whom? Such Christians can never do anyone any good. And as Nikabrik quickly learned, God does not exist to do our bidding. He does not require our belief to exercise His sovereign will, and if we're not careful—if we choose the object of our faith poorly—we might miss out on the ultimate victory celebration.

THE TEMPTATION OF POWER

Nikabrik's temptation to join the White Witch signifies more than just the allure of occult spirituality. Dwarfs are keen creatures; they don't miss much, and Nikabrik makes a telling comment during his confrontation with Caspian, Trufflehunter, and Dr. Cornelius, which shows he understands more about the nature of the White Witch than he first lets on. For all of their historical reputation, Peter, Susan, Edmund, and Lucy reigned for only a very short period of time before they disappeared. But the White Witch reigned for over a hundred years, keeping Narnia in the grip of winter for all that time. "There's power," Nikabrik said. "There's something practical."[8]

What attracts Nikabrik to the Witch is her power, or more precisely that she can be a means for him to have power. Though Nikabrik shares an honorable goal with the other Narnians, namely the defeat of King Miraz and the restoration of Old Narnia, he is seduced by power itself. This remains an occupational hazard for those who want to change the world.

Many postmodernists believe that all high ideals, all moral teachings, and all cultural institutions are nothing more than impositions of power. Whichever group has the power will construct paradigms to keep itself there. This is why Miraz tried so hard to cultivate a spirit of fear in his people regarding the myths of old—he wanted to maintain control over them. These postmodernists interpret all so-called cultural constructions—laws, morality, religion—in terms of men oppressing women, whites oppressing blacks, the rich oppressing the poor, heterosexuals oppressing homosexuals, and so on.

Today, political postmodernists use this argument as an indictment of what they see as various ruling classes. But the logic of this worldview is that your own group should seize power itself, if it can, and oppress the rest. Reducing *everything*—social customs, economics, the arts—to the pursuit of power is cynical and nihilistic in the extreme. Christians know there is a legitimate use of power; though they also know, especially in this fallen world, that power corrupts.

Unfortunately, Christians trying to influence their society in a positive manner often wage a "political war" instead. Politics is certainly an important arena, and Christians are right to get involved in political issues, get elected to public office, and push to get laws passed. But political power is not the same as cultural influence.

Over the last few decades, Christians have become adept at winning elections, wielding political clout, and seizing power. But while Christians were enjoying political success, the things our culture used to frown on—extramarital sex, homosexuality, living together, and having children outside of marriage—became perfectly acceptable. Christians were sitting in state legislatures passing laws, but the divorce rate—including among Christians—was soaring.

I by no means want to minimize the contributions of Christians in politics. We do need politicians and laws to protect human life, for example. But power only goes so far. A culture war must be fought in cultural terms. That means building up families, the basic unit of any human society. Cultural change must occur from within—from the bottom up rather than the top down. The weapons of this war are ideas, education, the media, the arts, books, music, movies. The same cultural forces that demolished traditional moral values must be used to rebuild them.

But pursuing political power is much easier. It is also more immediately gratifying. Yes, the pursuit of power can sometimes demand compromise and sacrifice morals, but to the victors go the spoils, and the trappings of power can be quite appealing: wealth, status, self-aggrandizement.

We can use power in a legitimate, moral way; but again, when human nature is involved, it can be difficult to honor good intentions. Few of us, if any, have the power to resist the Devil's temptations as Jesus did. And giving in, we often exercise our power at the expense of others, sometimes even those who are close to us. Husbands harm and demoralize their wives and families. Business executives take advantage of their employees and investors in the company. Even church leaders can lose sight of their ministries and focus instead on building empires.

But it does not have to be this way. We can rely on Jesus to help us navigate the muddy waters and to help us keep His principles foremost in our minds. Authority is real, and it has power. But as Jesus taught, we must use that power in love and service to our neighbors.

> You know that the rulers of the Gentiles lord it over them, and their great ones exercise authority over them. It shall not be so among you. But whoever would be great among you must be your servant, and whoever would be first among you must be your slave, even as the Son of Man came not to be served but to serve, and to give his life as a ransom for many. (Matt. 20:25–28)

Certainly Caspian was right to fight against tyranny, and surely his victory would have brought about positive changes. But could Prince Caspian, by his power alone, restore the old religion and make all the animals talk again? No, the landscape would have remained largely unchanged. The trees would still be silent, and the world would still be "wild." Replacing one king with another only establishes one thing: a new king. Righteous though he may be,

Prince Caspian could not have brought back Old Narnia on his own, and neither can we expect to change our world through political power or righteous might. To effect lasting change—the kind that matters—we need an entirely different kind of power: We need the supernatural power of Aslan, for that is the only power that can change human hearts.

THE TEMPTATION OF PRAGMATISM

But power in and of itself is oftentimes still not enough for most people. Nikabrik admired the White Witch's power because it was "practical." Trufflehunter's idealistic trust in Aslan was well and good, but it was not working. Nikabrik wanted results. And he would do anything to achieve them.

One philosophy that both modernists and postmodernists agree on is pragmatism. Modernist thinkers William James and John Dewey taught that, since the material world is the only criterion for truth, the test of an idea is its tangible, material usefulness. The postmodernist thinker Richard Rorty taught that, since truth is ultimately relative and unknowable, our only guide must be pragmatism, so that we act in a way that is useful for our goals. For pragmatists, "practical" considerations trump those old absolutes of what is true or good or beautiful.

The ethical corollary of pragmatism is "utilitarianism," which approaches morality not according to transcendent, objective absolutes (as in the Bible), but according to what is "useful." Instead of considering whether abortion is the murder of an innocent life, utilitarians look at the inconvenience a woman might experience if she has a baby, the practical consequences an unwanted child might have on her career or life plans, or even the consequences those circumstances might have on the baby itself. A utilitarian doesn't look at euthanasia in terms of how God values human life, but rather in terms of how much it costs to sustain the lives of terminally ill patients. The "greatest good" is of the utmost importance, but too often that good comes at a great expense to the few.

While nothing is wrong with practical considerations in general, pragmatism as an overarching philosophy and utilitarianism as an ethical system are incompatible with a Christian worldview. And yet, such is the cultural climate today that even Christians often succumb to pragmatism.

Church practices used to be determined on theological grounds. How a congregation would worship, what songs it would sing, and how ministry would be conducted—these were theological questions to be decided according to the church's understanding of Scripture. But now the major criterion in such matters may be often what "works." The goal is not necessarily to spread the gospel or even adhere to Scripture, but rather to get people in the door, whatever it takes, even if that means downplaying the doctrine of sin. Obviously people can't hear the gospel if they're not in the seats, but now the people who are in the seats sometimes can't hear the gospel either because the church is too busy trying to get people in the door. Pragmatism trumps theology.

For those of us trying to change the culture, like Nikabrik, "practicality" can become a subversive concern. It can divert us away from our true cause. The premodern Machiavelli, during the Renaissance, said that in the exercise of power, the ends do justify the means. The Prince, he said, must sometimes do evil—employ deception, eliminate enemies, lie, and be cruel—for the good of the state. This is political realism, Machiavelli argued, simply how the game must be played.

Unfortunately, even Christians often fall into this syndrome—not just in government, but also when they play office or church politics. And when they do, they look like hypocrites and turn others away from the message of the gospel.

What if Nikabrik had gotten what he wanted? What if the Old Narnians had brought back the White Witch? Perhaps she would have gotten rid of the Telmarines. But then what? Edmund could have told them. In *The Lion, the Witch and the Wardrobe*, the White Witch was quite solicitous in giving Edmund what he wanted—namely, a piece of Turkish Delight … oh, and revenge against the harsh treatment of his siblings. But in doing so she made Edmund her slave—she starved, bound, and dragged him behind her sleigh. Doubtless the Old Narnians would have won the day with the White Witch's help, but at what cost? Surely a decent ruler like Prince Caspian would not have been given the throne. Ironically, the Old Narnians would have replaced their ruthless tyrant with a dark queen. Bad means nearly always lead to bad ends. Pragmatism simply does not work.

THE DEFEAT OF TEMPTATION

Perhaps what is more important than temptations themselves, though, are the underlying factors that cause us to be susceptible to temptations in the first place. After all, anyone in his or her right mind wouldn't pay the slightest attention to the notion of getting in league with the Devil, or the White Witch, or whatever form he may take. We've all read the stories and know he means us nothing but harm. But there's the rub: We often aren't in our right minds when we are confronted with temptations that we would normally have nothing to do with.

It would be nice if reality were always shaded in black or white for us, but first and foremost we are human. Our moods, our emotions, and our circumstances all color our choices so they are not so easy to make. Some are still easy, to be sure. Most of us know we shouldn't rob a bank or start a fire. But what about when we feel tired or hurt or angry because of something that was done to us? Isn't it OK to lash out sometimes in the name of justice? Or to be selfish every once in a while when we feel like we've already given so much? And what about when we are faced with a choice we would rather not make? What if we have to shoplift or commit some other petty crime in order to feed our children? That's where the lines begin to blur, and that's where the Devil likes to lurk.

For instance, in *Prince Caspian* the Old Narnians are at the end of their rope. They feel they have tried everything in their power to rid themselves of the oppression of King Miraz, but nothing has worked—not even Queen Susan's horn, which they had been told would bring help. Readers know that help is on the way, but the Narnians themselves cannot see it, and so it means nothing to them. Nikabrik had been harsh toward Prince Caspian earlier in the story, and he has had a rather unpleasant attitude throughout most of the narrative, but it isn't until the Narnians have reached this point of despair that he truly gives in and considers, shall we say, less desirable means of victory.

But this is where Nikabrik makes his biggest mistake. So often it is at our lowest point that help is at hand—we just have to look for it. Jesus told us that the kingdom of heaven belongs to those who are poor in spirit and that the meek shall inherit the earth (see Matt. 5:3, 5), and Paul said that we should rejoice when we are weak for that is where we will find our greatest strength (see 2 Cor. 12:10). God does not intend to abandon us when we despair. Indeed, just like in *Prince Caspian*, He is probably standing right outside the door.

STUDY QUESTIONS

1. Do you know of people who started out on a journey or mission, only to find themselves corrupted along the way? These may have been a pastor of a church, a leader of a company, or just people looking to accomplish something through their own means.

What were the circumstances these people faced? Why do you think they failed? How did you react toward their decisions? How would the Bible prefer you to act in such circumstances in the future?

2. How do you view the relationship between faith and politics? Is there anything going on today that particularly interests you politically? What does the Bible have to say about your role as a Christian in such matters?

3. In what ways have you been, like Lewis, "desperately anxious to get rid of [your] religion"? Is this a good thing or a bad thing? Why or why not?

4. What do you think of the notion that many Christians nowadays "are dismissive of doctrines and concerned only with how God makes the feel"? That the focus of much of today's Christian teaching is on what is "comforting or exciting"? How is this different from cultivating Dionysian characteristics in faith, like we discussed in the last chapter? What does the Bible have to say about all this?

5. In your times of greatest need, do you rely on faith, or do you seek to accomplish your goals through your own means? (Be honest!) Study Matthew 5 and 2 Corinthians 12, and as you do so, pray and ask God for the strength and humility to live by faith, whatever that may look like in your present circumstances.

Nine

CALLING: HOW CULTURE
WARS ARE WON

*"I thought you'd come roaring in and frighten all the
enemies away—like last time. And now everything is
going to be horrid." ... Lucy buried her head in his
mane to hide from his face. But there must have been
magic in his mane. She could feel lion-strength
going into her. Quite suddenly she sat up.
"I'm sorry, Aslan," she said. "I'm ready now."
"Now you are a lioness," said Aslan, "and now all
Narnia will be renewed."*

—Lucy and Aslan, chapter 10

So how are the Old Narnians supposed to take back their country? More importantly, how can today's Christians influence
culture in a positive way? Christians today are often confused
about how they should relate to the world. Should we avoid it?
Conform to it? Take it over? Jesus says that we should be in the

world but not of the world (see John 17:15–18). But how can that be accomplished?

The Christian tradition has resources that can give direction for how Christ's followers can be salt and light in the world. One of the most important themes of the novel has to do with God's calling, known to Lewis as the doctrine of vocation. ("Vocation" is just a Latinate word for "calling.") This classic Christian teaching has nearly been forgotten in modern-day Christianity. But it is the key to how Christians can influence the culture as they once did.

C. S. Lewis said that *Prince Caspian* was about "restoring the true religion." Though we have used the metaphor of "culture war," we have discussed how the restoration of the true religion into a culture does not take place through a literal power struggle, whether military or political. But in our world, as in Narnia, cultural influence occurs when Christians hear the voice of God and live out their faith in their God-given vocations.

How God Works

The doctrine of vocation—explored most deeply in the writers of the Reformation, especially Martin Luther—teaches how God calls human beings into different relationships, roles, and realms of service.[1] God Himself works through the "vocations" of the human beings whom He has called. (Note that by "vocation" I am not just referring to someone's profession, though as you will see that can be a part of one's vocation.) For instance, God gives us this day our daily bread, as we pray in the Lord's Prayer, through the *vocation* of the farmer. God provides the food we need to sustain our lives through the vocations of the miller, the baker, the factory workers, the truck drivers, the stock boys, the woman at the checkout counter, and pretty much the rest of the economic system. Before we eat our meal, we thank God for our food, and it is right that we do so. But He gives us what we need through the labor of other people.

God performs an amazing miracle—the creation of new immortal lives—through the vocation of mothers and fathers. God is the one who gives life, but He does so by calling ordinary human beings into families. God proclaims and teaches His Word through ministers who have been called to preach it. He gives healing through the vocation of doctors, nurses, pharmacists, and other health-care professionals. He protects us through earthly governments, with their police officers, firefighters, military, and court systems. He teaches through teachers and creates works of beauty and meaning through artists. Every good and perfect gift comes from God, but He channels a good number of those gifts through other people.

Though God can and sometimes does work directly through miracles, He prefers to work through us. In particular, He chooses to work through human beings whom He has called to particular spheres of service. Vocation, said Luther, is God's mask. When we look at the face of the person who is doing something for us—the waiter who brings us our food at the restaurant, the garbage collector who hauls away our refuse, our parents who raised us—we should consider that God looms behind them. And He looms behind the talents, interests, and opportunities that He has given to ordinary people like you and me.

In *Prince Caspian*, Aslan acts to restore Narnia. But he does not do so directly, nor through the victory of superhuman heroes. He chooses instead to work through four ordinary English children.

CULTURE-SHAPING VOCATIONS

According to the doctrine of vocation, God calls people to faith, and He also calls people to different spheres of relationship and service in which they live out their lives on Earth. When God created human beings, He said it was not good for us to be alone and so ordained that we should live in families and then societies. And God exercises His sustaining care of human life through establishing particular institutions: the church, the family, the economic order, and the state. In these ordinary spheres of everyday life— which together constitute the culture—Christians are to live out their faith in love and service to their neighbors.

God established the family, which is the fundamental unit of every society. Marriage institutes a family, and being husbands and wives are divine callings from God. Being a father and being a mother are also callings, as is being a child, Luther said. Again, within the family, vocations are multiple. A woman might be the wife of her husband, the mother of her toddler, and the child of her parents. Other family relationships—brothers, sisters, uncles, aunts, nieces, nephews, cousins, grandparents—are also particular callings.

Peter, Susan, Edmund, and Lucy are members of the same family. In *The Lion, the Witch and the Wardrobe*, they are separated from their parents by war. While their father is in the military fighting Hitler, whose planes are bombing England's cities, their mother has sent them away into the country for their protection. Thus, both parents are carrying out their vocations by protecting their children, even though they are separated from them. In *Prince Caspian*, the children are again separated from their parents, this time because of the peculiar institution of the private English boarding school.

Both novels capture well the family dynamics of brother and sister relationships. They quarrel and they pull together, feel jealousy and family loyalty. Peter is the oldest, and both novels chronicle his attempts to face up to the responsibility of that calling, to supervise his younger brother and sisters, who in turn often resist his attempts to stand in for their father.

A central conflict in *The Lion, the Witch and the Wardrobe* was Edmund's rebellion against his calling in the family. He bitterly resented Peter and reacted against his authority. He also misused his own position as Lucy's older brother, mercilessly teasing and tormenting her. Edmund gave in to the White Witch, in part, because he wanted to vault over Peter. Such a sibling rivalry might seem minor, but in reality it was a function of Edmund's deep sinfulness. He betrayed his family, a profound sin against his vocation. But when Aslan died for him, Edmund was restored to his family, and his siblings welcomed back their prodigal brother.

Throughout these first books in the series, the family is the vocation in which the main characters, being children, exercise their spiritual and moral lives. They are too young to have jobs, as such, but as I alluded to earlier, Christians do have vocations in the workplace as well. Luther actually considered the workplace to be part of the family vocation, as in what a member of a family has to do to make a living for his household, the Latin word for which (*oeconomia*) gives us our word "economy." But, as we have gotten away from the family-based labor of the old farms and craftshops, we can now think of the workplace as a distinct calling. At any rate, it is evident that the different talents and abilities that people have—as well as their interests—are supplied by God to call us into a certain sphere of life that is unique for each of us. Indeed, the Bible's first explicit account of calling tells about how God called and equipped the artists whom He commissioned to make the art of the tabernacle:

> See, I have called by name Bezalel the son of Uri, son of Hur, of the tribe of Judah, and I have filled him with the Spirit of God, with ability and intelligence, with knowledge and all craftsmanship, to devise artistic designs, to work in gold, silver, and bronze, in cutting stones for setting, and in carving wood, to work in every craft. (Ex. 31:2–5)

Not only is the artist called personally to this work ("called by name"), but he is given the specific skills and capacities necessary to create works of art (ability, intelligence, knowledge, and craftsmanship).[2] From this we can deduce that the special abilities necessary to other callings—music, medicine, government, business—also come from God's hand.

Christians also have vocations in the state, or, more broadly, in the culture as a whole. God called us into particular communities, countries, and societies, at a particular time of history. Thus, we have a calling as citizens. Christians are right, according to the theologians of vocation, to take part in their government in order to ensure that the government is working according to its design.

In addition to the God-established institutions of church, household (the family plus its employment), and the state, Luther stressed that Christians also have callings in what he called "the general estate" or "the common order." He is referring here to the parts of our lives where people of all of the different vocations come together and interact—in other words, the common, everyday, unstructured parts of our lives. We are in the general estate when we are on our way to work, when we are enjoying our leisure, when we are interacting with our friends. This is the realm, Luther explained, of the Good Samaritan. The priest and the Levite were busy focusing on their own agendas, but they ignored the beaten and bloody traveler on the side of the road. The Samaritan, though, knew God was calling him to help his neighbor in need.

This underscores the purpose of every vocation, which is to love and serve one's neighbor. Christ revealed God's love to us through the ultimate act of service, and He wishes for us to do the same. But this cannot be accomplished through some splendid, monastic isolation that does not require us to interact with the messy world around us. Luther questioned the self-chosen pieties that people imagine they are doing for God but that do not actually help anyone. God does not need our good works, Luther emphasized, but our neighbor does. Luther's ethic was radically neighbor-centered, with Christians, motivated by God's love for them, living out their faith in free, generous service to others.[3]

We should continually ask what the young man asked Jesus,

"Who is my neighbor?" because the purpose of every vocation is to love and serve our neighbor. The answer to this question might be very different for different people. We have many different neighbors in our different vocations and in the various people who come into our lives. But in the specific calling of marriage, we each have only one neighbor to love and serve: our spouse. Wives are to love and serve their husbands (submitting to them as the church does to Christ, who is present in marriage), and husbands are to love and serve their wives (giving themselves up for them, as Christ did for the church). A parent's neighbor is his child, and parents show love to their children by serving them and taking care of them, by putting food on the table, taking them to church, driving them to soccer practice, and so on. (Luther said that changing a baby's diaper is a holier work than is done by all the monks in all the monasteries.) In the church, we are to love and serve our fellow members, not pick fights with them. In the workplace, our neighbors are our coworkers, superiors, and, above all, our customers, to whom our labor is directed. If a company no longer serves its neighbors' needs, it will soon go out of business and be replaced by one that does.

Where vocation can go wrong is clearly illustrated with King Miraz. As king, he has been given a particular authority and, with that, a particular responsibility. One of the clearest passages of Scripture on vocation is Romans 13:

> Let every person be subject to the governing
> authorities. For there is no authority except from
> God, and those that exist have been instituted by

> God. Therefore whoever resists the authorities
> resists what God has appointed, and those who
> resist will incur judgment. For rulers are not a ter-
> ror to good conduct, but to bad. Would you have
> no fear of the one who is in authority? Then do
> what is good, and you will receive his approval,
> for he is God's servant for your good. But if you
> do wrong, be afraid, for he does not bear the
> sword in vain. For he is the servant of God, an
> avenger who carries out God's wrath on the
> wrongdoer. (Rom. 13:1–4)

Human beings have no authority in and of themselves; only God does. But He exercises His authority by means of certain vocations, which include lawful rulers and also parents and other earthly authorities. Here we see how God works through human beings in their callings. The ruler is actually a servant—"God's servant"—an agent of God's judgment against evildoers. The calling of the ruler is to love and serve his neighbors, who are his subjects, by protecting those of "good" conduct and punishing those of "bad" conduct. In a fallen world, God must restrain the worst external excesses of sin, or human society would consume itself. He does so through earthly governments.

Romans 13, though, is often used to justify *any* governmental authority and to squelch dissent and political opposition. But that is surely a misreading and neglects the doctrine of vocation. A ruler's purpose is to exercise his office in love and service to his neighbor, specifically, to protect good citizens and to punish

wrongdoers. King Miraz, though, punishes good citizens and protects wrongdoers. God has not called him to do that. As a tyrant,
Miraz loves and serves himself, not his neighbors. God calls no one
to sin. Someone who uses a God-given calling for sinful purposes
has no authority from God.

We learn that King Miraz is actually a usurper, having killed
his brother, the true king. Prince Caspian, as rightful heir, is the
lawful king. The rebellion of the Old Narnians is not a revolution
against lawful authority. It is an attempt to restore it. Miraz is the
one who is violating Romans 13.

This doctrine of vocation is probably less glamorous than you
might have hoped, full of mundane, ordinary tasks. And so it is.
We much prefer our religion to be earthshaking and extraordinary.
As the Swedish theologian Einar Billing said, "In all our religious
and ethical life, we are given to an incredible overestimation of the
extraordinary at the expense of the ordinary."[4] The doctrine of
vocation transfigures the ordinary. It brings the fruits of faith into
every arena of life, into the way we actually spend our daily lives—
with our families, at work, in our leisure time—in all of its (to use
Lewis's term) "homeliness."

This Reformation doctrine of vocation stands against, of
course, that of medieval Catholicism, which taught that *only*
church work can be thought of as a calling from God. The call to
be a priest or a nun or a monk—with its vows of celibacy and
poverty—was once thought of as a sacred "vocation." It separated
a person from family and the economic life, which were considered
to be realms that, while necessary, fall short of spiritual perfection.
In contrast, according to Luther's doctrine of vocation, the family

and the workplace are "holy orders."[5] The hostile, sinful world itself is not something to flee from, as with monasticism. Rather, it, too, is a place for Christians who are called to that world to live out their faith. Through their vocations, Christians can interact with nonbelievers; thus, vocation becomes a means by which the world is evangelized. In vocation, Christians bring their faith into the public square, living out its implications in every institution and culture-affecting activity. Thus, vocation becomes a means by which Christianity can influence the world.

Ironically, in this modern and postmodern age, many evangelical Protestants have adopted the medieval Catholic view of vocation. They think only "spiritual" activities are worthy ways of serving God. They often minimize their own callings and so compartmentalize their lives, earning a living at their jobs while assuming the real spiritual action is in church on Sunday mornings or in small-group Bible studies. They might think their workday lives can be redeemed if they can witness to their coworkers and lead Bible studies during breaks. Though such religious activities on the job can indeed be a part of one's calling, these Christians often miss the sense in which *the proper labor of the job itself* can be a holy service.

Not that the doctrine of vocation necessarily simplifies things. Christians must often struggle to hear and accept God's calling. They must battle sin in vocation, such as the temptation to demand to be served rather than to serve and the temptation to work for the good of one's self rather than the good of one's neighbor. In our various callings, we often work against God's presence and His purpose. We also bear the cross in our vocations, experiencing futility, trials, and tribulations, which can drive us either to despair or to a deeper faith that comes from a closer dependence on Christ.

But the doctrine of vocation gives a Christian a very different perspective on ordinary life than that of nonbelievers. Did I choose my parents or my spouse or my country, or did God call me and place me in these relationships? In the common order of life, do I choose the tasks I want to do, or does God choose me for the tasks He wants me to do? Is the way I earn my living an "occupation" (meaning just something that keeps me busy) or a "vocation" (meaning something I have been called to)? In fact, some sociologists have noted that Protestants oftentimes have a stronger work ethic than their counterparts. This is not because the Puritans thought they had to prove their salvation by their prosperity, but rather because work itself acquired a new meaning for them.[6] This shows the power of the doctrine of vocation.

Does all of this sound new? Have you never heard this before? If this is the first time you have heard of what the doctrine of vocation consists of, that is evidence that contemporary Christianity has forgotten its most powerful culture-shaping tools. Christians interested in restoring the culture must recover the doctrine of vocation. This entails heeding God's call to service in every facet of life. *Prince Caspian* is a fantasy story, of course, with heroes fighting battles and performing other spectacular actions. But their victories hinge on the faithful performance of less-dramatic tasks: being a good brother or sister, assuming responsibilities, doing their duty, taking on the tasks that Aslan puts before them. By the same token, Christians wanting to change the culture do not necessarily have to seize political power. They can change the culture by living out their faith in their vocations: by building strong families, being active citizens, and using their God-given talents in every field.

LEWIS ON VOCATION

In "Learning in War-Time," a sermon addressed to students and scholars at Oxford as World War II was breaking out, Lewis takes up the question of what good comes from studying in the face of cataclysmic war. His answer is a meditation on vocation. He emphasizes how different vocations are equal before God, how each person's vocation is unique to him and a function of his gifts and circumstances:

> The work of a Beethoven, and the work of a char-woman, become spiritual on precisely the same condition, that of being offered to God, of being done humbly "as to the Lord." This does not, of course, mean that it is for anyone a mere toss-up whether he should sweep rooms or compose symphonies. A mole must dig to the glory of God and a cock must crow. We are members of one body, but differentiated members, each with his own vocation. A man's upbringing, his talents, his circumstances, are usually a tolerable index of his vocation.[7]

At that time and place, God had called those young people to serve at Oxford University, and the proper work of their calling was simply to study: "The learned life then is, for some, a duty. At the moment it looks as if it were your duty."[8]

Yes, their studies seem to be mundane in light of the struggle for civilization and survival itself, but this is the way of all vocations.

> I am well aware that there may seem to be an almost comic discrepancy between the high issues we have been considering and the immediate task you may be set down to, such as Anglo-Saxon sound laws or chemical formulae. But there is a similar shock awaiting us in every vocation—a young priest finds himself involved in choir retreats and a young subaltern in accounting for pots of jam.[9]

And yet, Lewis makes the case that the scholarly vocation *is* important for God's kingdom. Indeed, these Christian scholars play an important role in the intellectual and spiritual warfare that was the context of the struggle with fascism.

> To be ignorant and simple now—not to be able to meet the enemies on their own ground—would be to throw down our weapons, and then betray our uneducated brethren who have, under God, no defense but us against the intellectual attacks of the heathen. Good philosophy must exist, if for no other reason, because bad philosophy needs to be answered.[10]

Notice how Lewis is using the language of warfare (enemies, weapons, defense, attacks) to describe the conflict between Christianity and the "bad philosophy" of today's heathen.

In his fiction, Lewis often depicts ordinary people who are called to do their duty—a key concept in vocation, which Luther taught to the masses in the section of his catechism entitled "The Table of Duties"—or fulfill their role or do some simple task that turns out to have huge consequences. This often happens in Narnia. In *The Lion, the Witch and the Wardrobe*, we saw in both the breach and the performance the duties brothers and sisters owe to each other: Lucy realized her responsibility to her friend Tumnus; the White Witch's army had to be fought; the children had to assume their calling as kings and queens.

Lewis wrote another series of imaginative novels, the Space Trilogy, consisting not of fantasies for children but of science fiction for adults. These novels also explore spiritual issues through the projection of other worlds—though not through fantasylands in wardrobes as in The Chronicles of Narnia, but, rather, other planets. In *Perelandra*, Ransom, an ordinary philologist from Oxford—much like the audience of Lewis's "Learning in War-Time" sermon—finds himself in the precarious position of having to try to prevent another Eve on another planet from falling into sin (it is a rather long story as to *how* Ransom found himself in this position, to which I must simply suggest that you read the book):

> The fate of a world really depended on how they
> behaved in the next few hours.... What was the
> sense of so arranging things that anything really

important should finally and absolutely depend on such a man of straw as himself? And at that moment, far away on Earth, as he now could not help remembering, men were at war, and white-faced subalterns and freckled corporals who had but lately begun to shave, stood in horrible gaps or crawled forward in deadly darkness, awaking, like him, to the preposterous truth that all really depended on their actions; and far away in time, Horatius stood on the bridge, and Constantine settled in his mind whether he would or would not embrace the new religion, and Eve herself stood looking upon the forbidden fruit and the Heaven of Heavens waited for her decision.[11]

Ransom realizes that he has been brought to this planet by Maleldil (the Martian name for God) and called to this specific task to thwart the Tempter. "His journey to Perelandra was not a moral exercise, nor a sham fight," he concluded, realizing that God works through human beings. "If the issue lay in Maleldil's hands, Ransom and the Lady were those hands."[12] This is the doctrine of vocation.

The catch here is that we must not think we are capable of being God's hands on our own apart from Him. In *Prince Caspian*, Aslan asks Caspian if he feels sufficient to be the king of Narnia. With all sincerity, Caspian doesn't think so. "I'm only a kid," he says. To Aslan, this is the correct response. He replies, "If you had felt yourself sufficient, it would have been a proof that you were not."[13] The point is, we must not presume to live out our callings in our own strength, but in the strength of the Lord.

For Lewis, this is such an important aspect of how God accomplishes His work in this world. Surely God does not need our help to bring about change, but He chooses to let us in on what He is doing. In this way, we not only have a positive effect on the world around us, but we also feel closer to God ourselves. We feel like we are a part of something. Think about it: Have you ever been on a mission trip before? Weren't those tangible acts of service—whatever they may have been—much more fulfilling than simply giving money to your favorite charity? Didn't you feel much more energized in your faith afterward? But what Lewis is saying is that we don't have to go on a mission trip in order to have this experience—we can allow God to work through us in our everyday lives. And in doing so, we can have a larger impact on the world than we ever imagined possible.

STUDY QUESTIONS

1. What do you think of the notion that cultural influence occurs when Christians hear the voice of God and live out their faith in their God-given vocations? How are you doing in this? How can you get better at hearing God's voice?

2. How often do you look at the waiter who brings your food or the garbage collector who hauls the trash away and see the face of God? How might you be affected if you started viewing others like this with more regularity?

3. What are some of the God-given vocations you are fulfilling in your life right now? How might you be affected if you started viewing your own life as one of the means God is using to bless others? For instance, would you act differently in your relationship with your spouse if every moment you were thinking about how God would like to bless your wife or husband? How?

4. Who are your neighbors? Name them specifically. What could you do on a daily basis to treat them with the love and respect they deserve as your neighbors?

5. What do you think of this quote from Einar Billing: "In all our religious and ethical life, we are given to an incredible overestimation of the extraordinary at the expense of the ordinary"?

6. How might your life look different if not the main tasks, but rather the gaps in your life—traveling to and fro, running

errands, grabbing a snack—were seen as callings from God? How might this perspective affect how you see that other driver or the girl behind the counter at the coffee shop? Pray that God would expand your vision in this way and give you patience during the times you're not seeing so well.

Ten

FREEDOM: THE DIVINE REVEL

"What is it, Aslan?" said Lucy, her eyes dancing
and her feet wanting to dance.
"Come, children," said he. "Ride on my back again
today."
"Oh, lovely!" cried Lucy, and both girls climbed
onto the warm golden back as they had done no one
knew how many years before. Then the whole party
moved off—Aslan leading, Bacchus and his Maenads
leaping, rushing, and turning somersaults, the beasts
frisking around them, and Silenus and his donkey
bringing up the rear.

—chapter 14

As has been mentioned, Lewis the literary scholar said of Spenser's
The Faerie Queene, the pioneering allegorical Christian fantasy,
that each book, for all of its different adventures, contained a symbolic episode that was central to the meaning of each particular
book. Lewis the fantasy author used the same structure in his own

allegory, The Chronicles of Narnia. In the first book, *The Lion, the Witch and the Wardrobe*, the symbolic center is the sacrifice of Aslan on the Stone Table, followed by Aslan's resurrection from the dead. This, of course, symbolizes Christ's work of atonement.

In *Prince Caspian*, the symbolic high point is the "divine reveling" of Aslan and his company. "With leaping and dancing and singing, with music and laughter and roaring and barking and neighing,"[1] they roam the countryside, bringing release and freedom to everyone in bondage. This symbolizes the freedom and new life that Christ brings, the joyful Christian liberty that is the fruit of the gospel.

CHRISTIAN FREEDOM

Christianity is all about freedom, though this is perhaps not immediately obvious today. The fear of many non-Christians is that the Christian faith will not let them do what they want. Christianity does not approve of the sins they enjoy. Non-Christians know that if they become Christians, they will be expected to give up their sexual sins; they will have to put away their debauchery; they will have to put to death their pride, hedonism, and apathy.

And in this, the non-Christians are right. God does not tolerate sin. And what's more, the Christian life demands living for others instead of for oneself, being despised by the world, and bearing cross after cross. Jesus Himself told us this and warned that no one should become His disciple without counting the cost (see Luke 14:25–33). It may be worthwhile to live this kind of life, but to those who don't know it, it doesn't sound like freedom. And Christians do not very often act free either. We still struggle against our sinful proclivities. We often feel tempted by the freedom we think non-Christians have, and so we put restrictions on ourselves. We shield ourselves from non-Christians and their pursuits.

But this is not the life that Christ has called us to. The Bible exalts freedom. "For freedom Christ has set us free," says the apostle Paul. "Stand firm therefore, and do not submit again to a yoke of slavery" (Gal. 5:1). Why has Christ set us free? According to this passage, He set us free for freedom's sake. Freedom is not just a means to an end—freedom is both a means *and* an end. Christ gives freedom, and freedom is a sign of the Holy Spirit's presence. "Where the Spirit of the Lord is, there is freedom" (2 Cor. 3:17).

What the Bible means by freedom, however, is quite different— if not opposite—from what non-Christians mean by freedom. The latter want to be free *to sin.* The Bible teaches that sin is the enemy of freedom. Sin makes us slaves. Jesus Himself explained it best: "Jesus answered them, 'Truly, truly, I say to you, everyone who commits sin is a slave to sin. The slave does not remain in the house forever; the son remains forever. So if the Son sets you free, you will be free indeed'" (John 8:34–36).

The apostle Paul also talks about how sin enslaves us (see Rom. 6:16–22), but most of us don't have to read these words in the Bible to know they are true—we know from experience. An alcoholic is not free. Nor is a drug addict. Someone with an addiction to pornography or other sexual compulsion knows that he is in bondage. All sin, on some level, is like this. We cannot just "choose" to stop sinning. We might try to get rid of bad habits by sheer willpower, but what happens when our problem is precisely with our will?

One of Luther's classic books, *The Bondage of the Will,* makes the point that the human will is in bondage to sin. What we want—our deepest desires, yearnings, and lusts—is governed by sin. The struggle to improve our moral condition has to do with fighting these wants and desires. Our will, because of the fall, is in bondage to sin and the Devil and is in need of liberation.

And that is what Christ offers. He took what enslaves us— namely, sin—into Himself and put it to death on the cross. His sacrifice cancels the power of sin. His resurrection defeats the Devil. Christ has redeemed us, which is another way of saying that He has set us free. "So if the Son sets you free, you will be free indeed" (John 8:36).

When we have faith in this gospel, we are freed from sin. We are able to do what is right without imagining that we have to earn God's favor. Knowing that we are saved by grace and not by our own works, we are even freed from the law. Christ changes our lives and our attitudes so that we *want* to do what pleases Him. We may still sin sometimes, but we do not *want* to sin. Our wills have been released from their bondage. And when we are freed from sin, we can enjoy true freedom.

For most biblical writers, the notion that someone who is in thrall to sin might consider himself free would have been preposterous. But the disciple Peter understood this sophistry. Speaking of false prophets, he underscored the irony: "They promise them freedom, but they themselves are slaves of corruption. For whatever overcomes a person, to that he is enslaved" (2 Peter 2:19). He warns Christians not to slip into this mind-set themselves, while exhorting them to live as free people. "Live as people who are free, not using your freedom as a cover-up for evil, but living as servants of God" (1 Peter 2:16).

According to the apostle Paul, freedom is part of a Christian's calling. Freedom has to do with vocation, manifesting itself in what we do, not out of guilt or coercion, but out of the positive inner motivation of love. Because we know the love of Christ ourselves, we are enabled to love and serve our neighbors: "For you were called to freedom, brothers. Only do not use your freedom as an opportunity for the flesh, but through love serve one another. For the whole law is fulfilled in one word: 'You shall love your neighbor as yourself'" (Gal. 5:13–14). This passage recalls explicitly how the purpose of our callings is to love and serve our neighbors. And for those who have been liberated by Christ, this love and service become a joy rather than a burden.

THE LIBERATION STORIES

Thus salvation has to do with the movement from bondage to freedom. This is the teaching not only of Jesus and the apostles but also of the repeated narrative of the Old Testament.

The story of the children of Israel who became slaves in Egypt is central to the Old Testament. The pharaoh cruelly oppressed them, but God delivered them through Moses. By miracles, judgments, and ultimately the blood of the lamb, the Israelites crossed the Red Sea into freedom. Then God revealed Himself to them and gave them His commandments. Though many of the Jews rejected God in the wilderness and yearned to return to slavery because they felt their newfound freedom was too hard, God eventually brought His people into the land He had promised them.

Throughout the rest of the Old Testament, whenever God's people turned against Him by conforming to pagan cultures, practicing idolatry, falling into injustice, and committing other sins, they were given over to tyrannous kings, first from their own people and then from enemy nations. The people fall into bondage over and over again but then repent and are delivered as God sends someone to restore their freedom.

In the book of Judges, the Philistines control the Hebrew tribes until Samson liberates them at the cost of his own life. Gideon, Deborah, and other judges also liberate the people. In First and Second Kings, the people must suffer under rulers who do not do what is right in the Lord's eyes but also experience times of national freedom under righteous kings like David and Hezekiah. But sooner or later they fall into sin again, and God must send a prophet to call them to repentance. But during such times of trial—even when the people are carried away to Assyria and Babylon in captivity—God does not forget them and calls men like Daniel and Nehemiah to restore the nation. This ebb and flow of bondage and liberation, failure and redemption, is so repetitive, but it does have a purpose: It is a foreshadowing of the ultimate liberation to be found in Jesus Christ.

The great biblical drama of people in bondage being given their freedom through the efforts of a deliverer resonates throughout history as well. As Stanton Evans shows in his book *The Theme Is Freedom*, the Bible was profoundly influential in the development of political freedom.[2] It provided a higher moral law to which even kings were held accountable. The concept of the innate value and inalienable rights of individual human beings and the spiritual freedom available through the gospel would bear fruit in the political liberties of Western civilization. This progressed from the rejection of divinized emperors in the days of the early church, to the division of powers in the Middle Ages, to the rise of an educated and increasingly independent middle class after the Reformation, to the Protestant revolutions of the seventeenth century and the American Revolution of the eighteenth century.[3] And after that, the connection between Christianity and freedom manifested itself in the movements to abolish slavery, to increase human rights in the wake of Christian missions, and now to end such things as sex trafficking, genocide, and debilitating addictions.

C. S. Lewis also uses the metaphor of a revolution against a tyrant to symbolize the conflict between sin and grace. In *The Lion, the Witch and the Wardrobe*, the White Witch is a cruel despot who holds all of Narnia in her grip. This is an allusion to modern-day, real-world tyrants, such as the Nazis in World War II, whom the Pevensie children were fleeing in order to escape the German bombing raids in London. The White Witch even had "secret police," who took the form of a band of wolves. This is Lewis's way of symbolizing the reign of Satan on Earth. Just as the Witch keeps Narnia frozen in perpetual winter and turns her enemies into stone, so Satan seeks to harden our cold hearts by tempting us to sin. An underground movement—consisting of talking beavers, renegade fauns, and other Old Narnians—opposes her reign, but their rebellion is in vain until the death and resurrection of Aslan the lion.

Prince Caspian has a similar story line. Once again, Narnia is ruled by a tyrant whom a group of talking animals and other citizens of Old Narnia oppose in an underground movement. The Pevensie children are once again called to play a part in overthrowing this evil ruler, the difference being that, whereas the White Witch had supernatural powers, symbolizing Satan and his tyrannical rule over a fallen and sinful world, King Miraz is an earthly ruler who usurped the throne and did his best to stamp out belief in lions and the freedom that came with that belief. The White Witch was an emblem of a spiritual bondage; King Miraz is an emblem of a cultural bondage. But in both books, true freedom can only be found through Aslan.

Aslan's Romp

After Aslan rises from death in *The Lion, the Witch and the Wardrobe*, he and Lucy and Susan enjoy a "romp," a time of joyful play. That same word is used in *Prince Caspian* when Aslan reveals himself. Bacchus and his followers attend the lion and ask, "Is it a Romp, Aslan?"[4] whereupon the trees, the animals, and the maenads gather around Aslan and play. Lewis describes them as playing some combination of tag, hide the slipper, and blindman's bluff. But as they go, leaves sprout, vines spring up, and luscious grapes emerge. Yes, the imagery comes from Greek mythology, accompanying Dionysus, the god of wine. But the connection with Aslan, the symbol of Christ, points also to biblical imagery: Christ is the Vine. We are the branches. When we are in Christ, we can bear fruit (see John 15:1–6). And from the fruit of the vine comes the sacramental wine of the Lord's Supper, which Jesus describes as "my blood of the covenant" (Mark 14:22–25). Aslan's romp symbolizes the truth that Christ brings new life, freedom, and joy. "I came that they may have life and have it abundantly" (John 10:10).

We discussed Lewis's use of the Dionysian myth in chapter 7, but this context points to another dimension of this symbol. Dionysus had as his title "the liberator." In fact, the theater of Athens, the birthplace of Western drama, was named the theater of Dionysus *Eleutherios*, Dionysus the Liberator.[5] The pagan Greeks no doubt considered Dionysus liberating because of the way alcohol makes people shed their inhibitions—an example of a false view of freedom countered by Scripture. But in this context, with Aslan in control, the personification of liberation has a different meaning: the freedom that accompanies Christ the Liberator.

The romp begins when Aslan says, "We will make holiday."[6] The Christian custom of holidays—"holy days"—with the celebration and exhilaration that accompany festivals such as Christmas and Easter, is a sampling of the joy of Christ. The girls ride on the lion, who, accompanied by Dionysus, nontalking animals, and all the rest, begins his work of liberation.

From the beginning, the reveling is connected to liberation from bondage. The company first comes to the river, whose spirit hails Aslan and begs him to "loose my chains."[7] He is referring to the bridge that spans his waters. Aslan commands Dionysus to "deliver him." So ivy springs up, its tendrils wrapping around the stones of the bridge until the whole structure comes apart and falls into the water. The river is liberated. The episode relates also to another theme of the novel, the subjugation of nature. It is not just human beings who need to be released from their bondage. According to the apostle Paul, so does nature itself:

> For the creation was subjected to futility, not willingly, but because of him who subjected it, in hope that the creation itself will be set free from its bondage to corruption and obtain the freedom of the glory of the children of God. For we know that the whole creation has been groaning together in the pains of childbirth until now. (Rom. 8:20–22)

When Adam and Eve fell, they dragged nature down with them. The created order seemed futile, a realm of groaning and decay. This is because nature also is in "bondage" to sin and awaiting "the freedom of the glory of the children of God." What happens at the bridge represents how, through Aslan, the modernist no longer has control over nature.

Recall our discussion in chapter 6 of how modern thought, with its scientific dissections and technological manipulations, has reduced God's glorious creation to cold, lifeless material. Here the trees are awakening and the river speaks. Lewis is countering modernism with a vision of nature that is both ancient and apocalyptic. Aslan is delivering the very *land* of Narnia.

As Aslan and company continue their romp, the fabric of New Narnia comes further unraveled. When they come to a town, most people flee from their presence. But they soon come to a school that is full of girls who are not only wearing uncomfortable uniforms, but also have their hair pulled back tightly into buns. These details about clothing and hairstyle convey a sense of restriction. This, in turn, expresses what Lewis thought of the restrictive ideas taught in modernist schools. The students, he says, were having a history lesson. "The sort of 'history' taught in Narnia under Miraz's rule was duller than the truest history you ever read and less true than the most exciting adventure story."8

One of the students, Gwendolyn, looks out the window and excitedly exclaims that she sees a lion! Her teacher, Miss Prizzle, yells at her for such superstition. But then life breaks out in the classroom. At the approach of Aslan, ivy starts growing in from the windows, grass grows on the floor, and the teacher's desk turns into a rosebush. Miss Prizzle, seeing the lion, screams and runs away, along with most of the others; but Gwendolyn stays at Aslan's invitation and joyfully joins in the romp. She has found liberation.

Lewis obviously did not think much of modern, progressive education.9 Turning the exciting, inspiring tales of history into dull, lifeless "social studies" was merely a representative complaint. Lewis himself received a classical education, rich with ideas and imaginative stimulation.10 He studied history and books from all eras, freeing him, as we have seen, from the tyranny of fashionable thought. Progressive education, though, is in direct opposition to classical education. It minimizes tradition and downplays the value of the past, focusing on process rather than content and purporting to be scientific rather than philosophical. Progressive education thus instills the narrow, materialistic worldview that Lewis deplored. Lewis here is battling modernism, as fostered by modernist educational theory, but his same critique applies to today's postmodern educational theory, which turns against reason itself in favor of relativism, politics, and disdain for the "Old Western" heritage. For Lewis, what modernists did to nature, they also did to education: They restricted the wonder and joy that they should have inspired, and so education needs to be liberated.

In this vein, Lewis's friend J. R. R. Tolkien wrote an essay defending the value of fairy tales. Modernist literature, grounded in a worldview in which tangible matter is the only reality, was highly realistic. Modernists tended to look down on fantasy. Modernist educators followed suit, arguing that books for children should address only the reality of a child's world. Reading textbooks, generated by word frequency charts, were to venture no further than a few blocks from a typical child's home. Thus all the primers about Jack and Janet playing with their dog. They were purposefully written with a dull realism in which nothing of significance could happen, and the excitement of any kind of story or imaginative stimulation was systematically excluded.[11] As for fairy tales and fantasy in general, many progressive educators believed they were harmful for children. They condemned them as "escapist."

In his essay "On Fairy Stories," Tolkien made the point that if someone is in prison, it is healthy to want to escape.[12] According to Tolkien and Lewis, the materialistic worldview—with its stifling narrow-mindedness that leaves no room for God, the supernatural, or an individual's own spiritual yearnings—is a prison. Aslan delivers Gwendolyn from her soul-suffocating school, just as Christ must liberate our own minds.

But that's not all. Aslan also brings freedom from oppression. As the revels continue, animals of the nontalking sort break out of their bondage. Dogs break their chains and horses kick their carts to pieces and join the party. Then the company comes upon a man beating a little boy. But at the approach of Aslan, the stick turns into a flower. The abuser tries to throw it down, but it sticks to his hand, which turns into a branch. He himself turns into a tree. The boy's crying turns to laughter, and he joins the celebrating throng.

Soon they come to another school. This time a boys' school populated by mean little lads with piglike faces. This time it is the teacher who needs deliverance. She is a sensitive young woman, whose class runs all over her and couldn't care less about learning anything. She is tired and discouraged, burnt out from having to struggle against a culture that cares nothing for high ideals but only for indulging its appetites (hence the "pig" descriptions). She looks out the window and sees something more: Aslan and his "divine revelers." Seeing them, "a stab of joy [goes] through her heart."[13] This recalls Lewis's own experiences of transcendence that he described in *Surprised by Joy*. Her students cannot even see Aslan, and they berate their teacher and threaten to report her to the authorities. But Aslan stops under the window, looks up at the teacher, and calls to her. She jumps out the window to join the romp just as her students turn into actual pigs.

But the ultimate liberation Christ offers is yet to come. Aslan and his revelers come to a cottage where they see a little girl crying. Her aunt is dying. Aslan goes into the little cottage, though he is too big for it. He pushes his head through the door and ends up lifting the whole house on his back. The point is that Aslan is so much bigger than human constructions. The old woman, lying on her bed, which is now in the open air, recognizes Aslan. She greets him, confessing her faith by saying she knew that he was real and that she had been waiting for him all of her life. She asks if Aslan is going to take her away now. The lion says that he is, but not on the long journey that comes after death. Instead, he heals her.

Lewis takes this opportunity to tie up a thread in the plot. It turns out that the woman is Caspian's old nurse, who first told him about Aslan and Old Narnia. Miraz made her disappear, but we readers get a sense of resurrection when we learn that she is alive after all. Aslan delivers her from her physical bondage to sickness and, in a sense, from her bondage to mortality—which is to say, Christ liberates us even from death.

Finally, Aslan's romp joins the main plot when the joyful throng comes to the battlefield. Peter's single-combat duel with Miraz degenerates into a free-for-all battle with the Telmarines. But Aslan and his freed followers put an end to it. When the Telmarines see the woods moving toward them and Aslan's awakened trees attacking, they panic and run away.[14] The Old Narnians overthrow the Telmarines, but the victory belongs to Aslan. Narnia is free.

STUDY QUESTIONS

1. Why is it that Christians rarely *act* free? Why do we still struggle against our sinful proclivities? Why is the apparent "freedom" that non-Christians have so appealing?

2. What would it look like to you to live as though you are free? How would this affect your attitude toward God and others?

3. What do you think of the notion that the Jews rejected God in the wilderness and yearned to return to slavery because they felt their newfound freedom was too hard? In what ways can you resonate with their perspective?

4. What, if anything, in your life reflects the joyful "romp" of Aslan and his cohorts? Where does their joy come from? How can you find more of that joy in your own life? If there is any one thing you should take away from this book, it is that your relationship with God should be filled with joy. Pray to God for this, and that others would experience that joy as well.

CONCLUSION
RESTORING CHRISTENDOM

"Men of Telmar," said Aslan, "you who seek a new land,
hear my words. I will send you all to your own country,
which I know and you do not."
—chapter 15

When Caspian first fell in with the Old Narnians, the company was bickering. The badger Trufflehunter had faith in Aslan, but Nikabrik was willing to believe in anybody or anything that would help him drive out the hated Telmarines. It didn't matter to him. He was open to religion, but only as a means to his own ends. He didn't care about the content of the religion as long as it helped him accomplish what he wanted. Trumpkin, on the other hand, didn't believe in Aslan but still objected to allying himself with the White Witch on moral grounds. Caspian, though he had just been anointed king by the Old Narnians, didn't really know what to do. That's when a centaur named Glenstorm came up and asked a simple question: When are we starting the war?

> Up till now neither Caspian nor the others had
> really been thinking of a war. They had some vague
> idea, perhaps, of an occasional raid on some human
> farmstead or of attacking a party of hunters, if it
> ventured too far into these southern wilds. But, in
> the mean, they had thought only of living to them-
> selves in woods and caves and building up an
> attempt at Old Narnia in hiding.[1]

Christians in our world, who chafe at the "New West" with its
secularism and materialism, are in a similar dilemma. Should we let
the culture run rampant and just withdraw into our caves? Should we
try to build up some kind of Christian culture, an "Old Western" civilization of our own, apart from the culture around us? Could we just
make raids on modern and postmodern culture, occasionally winning
a victory here and there, and then go back into hiding? Or should we
engage today's culture, hostile to our faith though it is, and try to
bring back a Christian influence to bear on the culture as a whole?

What does it even mean to start a "culture war"? It is impossible
to restore Christianity to the culture through a literal war. Armed
combat may sometimes be necessary against naked aggression in this
world, but it usually only results in one side attaining power over
another. Christianity has to do with faith, which can never be
coerced or forced on anyone. Therefore, the warfare imagery in
Prince Caspian must be symbolic, but what it symbolizes is real.

After the centaur Glenstorm brings up the subject, Caspian and
the Old Narnians agree that they must fight Miraz and not merely
hide from him. The issue, though, is not whether or not they will

win. Rather, they come to feel that they have a *duty* to enter the conflict. "It now seemed to them quite possible that they might win a war and quite certain that they must wage one."[2]

The message from *Prince Caspian* for today's Christians is that we must not run away from intellectual, moral, and spiritual combat. We have a duty to stand our ground and do what we can. Ultimately, though, we cannot win this war by ourselves, as the Old Narnians learned. We must rely on God to work through us in order to "restore the true religion," which is what Lewis himself proclaimed as the main theme of *Prince Caspian*.

THE HAPPY ENDING

But that doesn't mean that we should just sit back and do nothing. The ending of *Prince Caspian* illustrates the necessity of personal fortitude during times of cultural conflict. The book does not portray the Old Narnians rising up victoriously. The Old Narnians are *losing*. The Telmarines are beating them in battle. In fact, they reach such a low point, are so unsuccessful, that they are tempted to turn to the powers of the Witch. Even the arrival of the Pevensie children does not solve their problems. Outnumbered and overwhelmed, High King Peter takes command and says that he believes Aslan is near, though he does not know when the lion will act. In the meantime, Peter concludes, Aslan would simply like them to do what they can.

This is a major theme of the resolution of the story: Peter decides to try to settle the war through hand-to-hand combat and proposes to fight Miraz alone. As it turns out, they are quite evenly matched. The duel goes back and forth—sometimes Peter has the advantage, while other times Miraz takes the upper hand.

Eventually Peter becomes exhausted. He sprains his wrist and can scarcely hold his shield. At one point, thinking he's about to die, he even says farewell to Edmund and Dr. Cornelius, but he courageously carries on the fight. And this is the point: Though the outcome is uncertain, Peter carries out his calling. Faithfully fulfilling the responsibilities of our calling does not necessarily guarantee success, but then that is the nature of acting in faith.

When we face failure, we are often tempted to compromise our principles in order to avert disaster. At one point during the duel, Miraz trips and falls. Peter refuses to take advantage, though, and steps back in a demonstration of integrity to allow his enemy to stand up again. Edmund regrets Peter's generous act of chivalry but realizes that this is what Aslan would have wanted Peter to do. Peter would rather die than win dishonorably. He knows that, no matter what his own fate might be, the ends do not justify the means.

Apart from Aslan's intervention, though, the most these "culture warriors" can achieve is utter chaos. They can achieve no real lasting success on their own—though their victories might delay the enemy's advances just a little bit longer. Thankfully for the Old Narnians, though, evil often trips itself up of its own accord.

Hoping to seize power for themselves, two Telmarine officers had manipulated Miraz into accepting the duel with Peter in the first place. When the duel is stalemated, these same Telmarines rush the field and stab Miraz themselves. Bad people turn against each other. Unrestrained evil burns itself out. And yet, the battle keeps raging. The problem was never just the rule of one bad man, but a Telmarine mind-set that went far deeper. Miraz may be dead, but now on the battlefield what reigns is chaos, and the Old Narnians are still losing.

What finally turns the battle in Narnia's favor is Aslan's romp. Not only is Aslan accompanied by all kinds of ancient creatures, but he has now awakened the trees, and for the Telmarines, this is a terrifying sight. Can you imagine how you would react if you saw a forest moving and coming at you? The Telmarine army panics, understandably, and flees to the river, but the bridge it had hoped to escape over is no longer there. It is the same river that Aslan had freed from its restraints earlier in the story. The Telmarines are trapped.

But it is not just the effects of Aslan's revelation but, very specifically, his presence. When Aslan finally arrives at the battleground along with his company of divine revelers, the terror-stricken Telmarines fall on their faces. "They had not believed in lions and this made their fear greater."[3] Not only that, the atheists on the Old Narnian side feel the same way. The dwarfs who were skeptical about the existence of lions, like Trumpkin, also draw away. The talking animals, on the other hand, gather round Aslan, snuffling him, rubbing against him, and expressing their affection according to their own natures. The image represents the glory of Christ's return: Some will be terrified at His approach. Others will welcome the coming of their Lord.

But all is not lost for the Telmarines. For though they are sinners and always have been (as we learned from their past as pirates), they are nonetheless Sons of Adam and Daughters of Eve and therefore the rightful rulers of Narnia, for Narnia is not complete without a Son of Adam or a Daughter of Eve on the throne. Many of the Telmarines believe that Aslan will kill them, but instead he shows them mercy. Those who wish to stay in Narnia can, and the others will be sent back to their original island on Earth.

This is not, however, a last judgment. Going back to Earth is not the same as going to hell. We see one Telmarine on his way back to Earth who trusts Aslan, who then breathes on him (symbolizing the Holy Spirit) and sends him through with a blessing. Their original island is now uninhabited and fruitful. It's as if those going back have been given a new lease on life—a chance to build a new civilization the right way. Still, most of the Telmarines are fearful. But Peter, Susan, Edmund, and Lucy realize that they, too, need to go back; and if they take the lead, the rest of the Telmarines will follow. They put their school clothes back on, make their farewells, and walk through the doorway Aslan created. The next thing they know, they are back in England at the railway station, at the same moment they had been whisked away. They bask in the ordinary sights and the familiar atmosphere. They are glad to be back, even though they have to go back to school.

THE WORK OF ASLAN

So what is the point of this happy ending? The restoration of the true religion is all Aslan's doing. Just as Aslan achieved the victory over the White Witch in *The Lion, the Witch and the Wardrobe*, he achieved the victory over New Narnia in *Prince Caspian*. This symbolizes the truth in our world that Christ does it all: He convicts us of our wrongdoing, He calls us to Himself through His Word, He saves us through His death and resurrection, He sanctifies us through His work in our lives, and He rules over heaven and Earth. And if He chooses to "restore the true religion" in our culture, He will do that.

In *Prince Caspian*, individuals do not bring back Old Narnia. They each play their own part, to be sure, but are eventually defeated one way or another: Caspian's old nurse is driven away. Dr. Cornelius must flee for his life. The Old Narnian resistance, once it gets past its constant bickering and its temptations to seize power in the wrong way, is defeated in battle. Peter fights bravely, but his duel with Miraz ends in a draw—and very well could have ended worse had the other Telmarines not interfered. They accomplish nothing good or lasting until Aslan comes.

The signature moment that dramatizes the futility of human self-sufficiency comes when the Pevensie children trust their own instincts as they look for a way through the forest. Predictably, they get hopelessly lost. If it weren't for the trusted guidance of Aslan's word (since none but Lucy could see him yet), they might have never joined the fight against Miraz.

And just as Aslan worked through Lucy in that situation, he worked through other individuals as they lived out their faith according to their callings. The old nurse told the young prince about Aslan and the tales of Old Narnia. Caspian's teacher, Dr. Cornelius, had the historian's integrity to tell him the truth about the past. Lucy, Edmund, Susan, and Peter are schoolchildren, but they accepted their responsibilities as kings and queens of Narnia.

But perhaps the most important calling of the whole story is that of Prince Caspian. The prince, at first a confused young boy, entered his calling as the rightful king and took charge of the disorganized Narnian resistance. It is important, though, to notice that this is not really a rebellion, much less a revolution. At first, the underground movement bears those marks. It is reactionary, opposed to the Telmarine rule, but without a clear view of what it would put in its place. Dwarfs like Nikabrik are motivated mainly by hatred and would employ *any* ideology or tactic—good or evil—that would rid Narnia of these alien occupiers.

But when they find Prince Caspian, the resistance crystallizes around a new cause, and as it does so, it changes. The problem with King Miraz is not that he is a Telmarine, but that he is really not a king. Miraz usurped the throne by killing the former king, his own brother. Miraz has no calling to be king. This is not his vocation.

By law, when a king dies—whether of old age or, as in this case, by murder—his son succeeds him to the throne. That would be Caspian. Now Miraz seeks to kill *him* to secure his own ill-gotten crown. But when the Old Narnians accept Caspian as their king and decide to wage war against the illegitimate regime, they are acknowledging the rule of law. They are fighting to uphold the law, not to break it. They are supporting lawful government, not rebelling against it. Miraz is the real rebel against lawful authority.

The Old Narnians are no longer trying to overthrow the Telmarines, as such. Caspian is a Telmarine. He, too, descended from castaway pirates, who blundered their way from Earth into Narnia. His difference with the New Narnians, though, is that Caspian has different ideas, a different spirit. He believes in Aslan. And Aslan has called him to be king and to preside over the restoration of Narnia.

RESTORING OUR WORLD

Throughout this book, we have drawn out the parallels between the Narnians, both new and old, and our own contemporary culture. In

Prince Caspian, Lewis uses fiction to carry out the same critiques against our post-Christian age that he champions in his nonfiction books. The New Narnians have forgotten Aslan; our world has forgotten Christ. As a result, both have embraced a stifling, narrow worldview with no room for moral ideals, transcendent wonder, or genuine freedom.

At the end of *Prince Caspian,* Narnia is restored. As we saw earlier, this volume in The Chronicles of Narnia shows the "restoration of the true religion after corruption."[4] So what lessons can we learn from this story about the restoration of the true religion in the real world today?

Evangelical Christians have doctrinal differences in the way they approach the question of how and to what extent Christians should interact with the secular world. Some believe that our culture will continue to spiral downward until the day of the Antichrist, so there is not much we can do to improve society until Christ returns. Others believe that it is up to us to establish the thousand-year reign during which Christ will return, and we must take control of our culture to do so.

Lewis, though, approaches the issue from a different angle altogether. His own theology of cultural engagement seems to go something like this: Yes, the restoration of the true religion and the restoration of the culture depend on the coming of Christ. But Christ doesn't just come at the end of time. He is already present in His Word, sacramentally in His church, in His providential sovereignty, and in the lives of His people. Yes, things might get worse for Christians, whose influence may keep dwindling in a world that grows ever further from God. But we must remain faithful, remembering Christ and following His Word, and, as Peter says, do what we can. Christians should await Christ's coming by staying at their posts, making productive use of their talents, and loving and serving their neighbors in whom Christ is hidden.

That is to say, no matter what the future may hold, we are expected to exercise our God-given *vocations*. We are to live out our faith in Christ in our God-given callings. Tending to these callings is how we can exercise a godly influence on our culture.

Some Christians are called to the political arena, whether as activists or as rulers (Lewis's preferred term for "leaders").[5] All Christians have a calling as citizens, with the responsibilities that entails, such as voting. Romans 13 describes how God is at work through the legal governmental authorities to punish evildoers and to protect those who do well.

Government alone, however, does not dictate culture, and political power is not enough to change the moral and spiritual condition of a society. The callings that have the most cultural importance are the family vocations. After all, as all sociologists and anthropologists agree, the basic unit of any culture is the family. Therefore, the surest way for Christians to have an impact on the culture is to build strong Christian families.

This means recovering marriage as a Christian vocation. Instead of blindly conforming to modern culture's view of marriage, with its sentimental romanticism and openness to divorce, Christian men and women must see marriage as a divine calling, in which spouses, like Christ and the church, love and serve each other.

This also means recovering parenthood as a Christian vocation. Instead of following modern society's mode of parenting in which children are essentially abandoned to be raised by their peers, Christian parents must love and serve their children in accordance with the nurturing work of our Father in heaven.

This also means recovering childhood as a Christian vocation. Instead of always rebelling against our parents, which includes rebelling against the traditions of our forebears, we must honor our fathers and our mothers.

Christians may feel they have little control over cultural institutions, but the church is still one of the most effective institutions in today's world. We need to recover life in the church as a Christian vocation. Instead of conforming to the dominant culture, the church should cultivate a culture of its own, becoming an intimate spiritual community that values both the unity and the diversity of the body of Christ.

Christians need to recover the sense in which their different talents and interests, the opportunities they have, and the ways they make a living are callings from God. We need Christians in every niche of the culture. We need Christians in farms, factories, small towns, suburbs, and big cities. We need Christians in business, engineering, science, and the media. We need Christians to pursue callings in the entertainment industry—in film, television, and music—and in the arts, fields that have a special impact in shaping people's tastes, ideas, and morals.

We need Christian scholars in every field. Nudging the dominant worldviews in a more biblical direction requires action on a number of different fronts. As Lewis himself said, "What we want is not more little books about Christianity, but more little books by Christians on other subjects—with their Christianity *latent*."6

Because postmodernism is inherently anti-intellectual (meaning it values subjective truth more than objective truth), Christians have an opportunity to advance into positions that can have an influence on learning. With the accelerating decline of secularist education, Christians—in their homeschools, academies, and colleges—are poised to become the best-educated (and thus the most culturally influential) members of society.

In this way, Christians can fulfill their calling to be salt and light to the world around them. We don't have to be dramatic or do anything earth shattering to have an impact, for it is in the realm of the ordinary that most of life takes place. The ordinary, in fact, is one of the most important spiritual realms. In another of Lewis's symbolic fantasies, *The Great Divorce*, one of the greatest saints in heaven is Sarah Smith of Golders Green, an ordinary woman no one has heard of, who casts a spiritual influence on her family, the people she meets, and even on the animals she sees.[7]

Prince Caspian is a wonder-filled fantasy, but ultimately it celebrates what ordinary individuals can accomplish when they honor their callings. Caspian's nurse tells him about Aslan. Dr. Cornelius does his job as a history teacher. The Narnians blow the horn when they think they need to. Four ordinary schoolchildren follow the path that is laid before them. And Aslan—the Christ—does the rest.

NOTES

INTRODUCTION
1. George Sayer, *Jack: A Life of C. S. Lewis* (Wheaton, IL: Crossway, 1994), 315–16.

2. Ibid.

3. Ibid., 313.

4. Ted Baehr, who found the letter, quotes it in his book *Narnia Beckons: C. S. Lewis's The Lion, the Witch and the Wardrobe and Beyond* (Nashville: Broadman & Holman, 2005), 17.

5. The title of one of his essays published in 1956, collected in *Of Other Worlds: Essays and Stories*, ed. Walter Hooper (London: Geoffrey Bles, 1966).

CHAPTER 1
1. Sayer, *Jack*, 314.

2. Ibid., 315.

3. In *Of Other Worlds.*

4. A good introduction to worldview analysis is James Sire, *The Universe Next Door: A Basic Worldview Catalog* (Downers Grove, IL: InterVarsity Press, 2004).

5. John Calvin, "Argument," *Commentary on Genesis*, trans. John King (London: Billings & Son, 1975). Calvin also uses this metaphor in *The Institutes*, Book I, Chapter 6.

6. See Francis Schaeffer, *Escape from Reason* (Downers Grove, IL: InterVarsity Press, 1968).

7. G. K. Chesterton, *Orthodoxy* (New York: Doubleday, 1959), 9–10.

8. Ibid., 11.

9. Victor Shklovsky, "Art as Technique," trans. Lee T. Lemon and Marion J. Reis,

in David Lodge, ed., *Modern Criticism and Theory: A Reader* (London: Longmans, 1988), 16–30.

10. Ibid.

11. See my book on the all-but-lost doctrine of vocation, *God at Work: Your Christian Vocation in All of Life* (Wheaton, IL: Crossway, 2002).

12. G. K. Chesterton, *Heretics* (Charleston, SC: BiblioBazaar, 2006), 27.

13. *The Soul of the Lion, the Witch and the Wardrobe* (Colorado Springs: Victor Books, David C. Cook, 2005), 12–14.

14. C. S. Lewis, *Mere Christianity* (New York: HarperCollins, 2001), 52.

15. "Sometimes Fairy Stories May Say Best What's to Be Said," in *Of Other Worlds*, 37.

CHAPTER 2

1. Lewis worked out the chronology of the different stories in a manuscript entitled "Outline of Narnian History," which was published by Walter Hooper in his essay "Past Watchful Dragons: The Fairy Tales of C. S. Lewis," in *Imagination and the Spirit: Essays in Literature and the Christian Faith Presented to Clyde S. Kilby*, ed. Charles A. Huttar (Grand Rapids, MI: Eerdmans, 1971), 298–301.

2. C. S. Lewis, *Prince Caspian* (New York: Collier Books, 1970), 53.

3. Alexander Pope, "Epitaph. Intended for Sir Isaac Newton, in Westminster-Abbey," in *The Oxford Book of English Verse*, ed. Christopher Ricks (New York: Oxford University Press, 1999), 266.

4. C. S. Lewis, "Is Theology Poetry?" in *The Weight of Glory* (New York: Macmillan, 1980), 90.

5. C. S. Lewis, *"De Descriptione Temporum,"* in *They Asked for a Paper* (London: Geoffrey Bles, 1962), 9–25. Posted at http://www.eng.uc.edu/~dwschae/temporum.html.

6. C. S. Lewis, *The Discarded Image* (New York: Cambridge University Press, 1964), 220.

7. Ibid., 221.

8. C. S. Lewis, *Surprised by Joy* (New York: Harcourt Brace Jovanovich, 1956), 207–8.

9. Chesterton, *Orthodoxy*, 74–75.

10. C. S. Lewis, "Vivisection," in *God in the Dock*, ed. Walter Hooper (Grand Rapids, MI: Eerdmans, 1970), 227.

11. Ibid., 228.

12. *Prince Caspian*, 60.

13. C. S. Lewis, "The Future of Forestry," in *Poems*, ed. Walter Hooper (New York: Harcourt Brace Jovanovich, 1964), 63.

CHAPTER 3
1. *Prince Caspian,* 50.

2. Ibid., 72.

3. C. S. Lewis, "On the Reading of Old Books," in *God in the Dock,* ed. Walter Hooper (Grand Rapids, MI: Eerdmans, 1970), 200–207.

4. Sayer, 227–232. According to Sayer, 226, Lewis became a Christian on September 22, 1931. He wrote *Pilgrim's Regress* in August 1932.

5. William Wordsworth, "Lines Composed a Few Miles above Tintern Abbey," l. 49, in *Oxford Book of English Verse*, 344.

6. William Wordsworth, "The Tables Turned," l. 28, in *The Norton Anthology of English Poetry*, 4th ed., ed. M. H. Abrams. (New York: W. W. Norton, 1976), 2:154.

7. T. S. Eliot, "Metaphysical Poetry," in *Selected Prose*, ed. Frank Kermode (New York: Harvest, 1975), 59–67.

8. Ibid.

9. Ibid.

10. See Sayer, 258.

CHAPTER 4

1. Nancy Pearcey, *Total Truth: Liberating Christianity from Its Cultural Captivity* (Wheaton, IL: Crossway Books, 2004).

2. See Alvin J. Schmidt, *How Christianity Changed the World* (Grand Rapids, MI: Zondervan, 2004). The earlier title was *Under the Influence: How Christianity Transformed Civilization.*

3. *Prince Caspian*, 40.

4. German has a word for this, cited by Lewis: *Sehnsucht,* the word for "longing," which derives from the word for vision and the word for searching.

5. *Prince Caspian*, 50.

6. Ibid., 51.

7. *Surprised by Joy,* 132–46. See also Sayer, *Jack*, 92–95.

8. See *Prince Caspian,* 72.

9. *Prince Caspian*, 66.

10. See Ayn Rand, *The Virtue of Selfishness* (New York: Signet, 1964).

CHAPTER 5

1. *Prince Caspian*, 121.

2. "Living on the Edge of Faith: Daily Success Motivation and Positive Thinking." Upgrade Your Mind. Accessed April 21, 2007. http://thinkblade.typepad.com/upgradeyourmind/2005/02/living_at_the_e.html.

3. Actually, Kierkegaard's phrase, from *The Concept of Anxiety,* was "a leap to faith." He was referring to the transition from Christian unbelief to belief. Of course, in making "faith" the object of faith—rather than faith in the crucified Jesus—he contributed to religious subjectivity.

4. *Prince Caspian,* 136.

5. Ibid.

6. Ibid., 138.

7. Ibid.

8. Ibid., 143.

9. Ibid., 144.

10. C. S. Lewis, *Mere Christianity* (New York: HarperCollins, 2001), 131.

CHAPTER 6

1. See Sayer, *Jack*, 49–50, and *Surprised by Joy*, 13–16.

2. J. R. R. Tolkien, "On Fairy-Stories" in *The Monster and the Critics and Other Essays* (New York: HarperCollins, 1997).

3. Full citation chapter 2 #8, *Surprised by Joy*, 15.

4. Ibid., 7.

5. Ibid., 16.

6. Ibid., 16–17.

7. Ibid., 17.

8. Ibid., 152.

9. From Carl Sagan's documentary series *The Cosmos* (PBS).

10. William Shakespeare, *Hamlet*, Act II, scene ii, line 263.

11. *Prince Caspian*. 60.

12. William Wordsworth, "The Tables Turned," l. 28, *Norton Anthology*, 2:154.

13. William Blake, "And Did Those Feet in Ancient Time," l. 8 in Preface to *Milton*, in *The Selected Poetry of William Blake* (London: Wordsworth Editions, 1993), 319.

14. Gerard Manley Hopkins, "God's Grandeur," ll6–7, in *Norton Anthology of English Literature*, 2:1789.

15. *Prince Caspian*, 76.

16. Ibid., 79.

17. Ibid., 172–73.

18. Ibid., 135.

19. See the final stanza of Dante's *Paradise.*

20. *Prince Caspian,* 65.

21. Ibid., 66.

22. Ibid., 212.

23. Ibid., 117.

CHAPTER 7

1. *Prince Caspian,* 152.

2. See David C. Downey, *Into the Wardrobe: C. S. Lewis and the Narnia Chronicles* (San Francisco: Jossey-Bass, 2005), 149–50; and Humphrey Carpenter, *Tolkien: A Biography* (New York: Ballentine, 1977), 227.

3. See his book *Spenser's Images of Life* (Cambridge: Cambridge University Press, 1978). The book that made Lewis's scholarly reputation and that treats Spenser in ways that point ahead to what Lewis himself attempted to do with Narnia is *The Allegory of Love* (Oxford: Oxford University Press, 1936).

4. *The Allegory of Love,* 166.

5. See my book *Classical Education,* written with Andrew Kern (Washington, D.C.: Capital Research Center, 2001).

6. Lewis details his own classical education throughout *Surprised by Joy.* For the importance of classical languages and literature in Western civilization—including how Christians used them—see E. Christian Kopff, *The Devil Knows Latin: Why America Needs the Classical Tradition* (Washington, D.C.: ISI Books, 2000).

7. See Werner Jaeger, *Paideia: The Ideals of Greek Culture,* trans. Gilbert Highet (New York: Oxford University Press, 1965), xxvii–xxviii.

8. *"De Descriptione Temporum."*

9. Ibid.

10. Ibid.

11. *Surprised by Joy*, 228.

12. Sayer, *Jack*, 225–26.

13. *Surprised by Joy*, 236.

14. Ibid., 226.

15. Ibid.

16. Ibid., 237.

17. C. S. Lewis, "Myth Became Fact" (1944), in *God in the Dock: Essays on Theology and Ethics,* ed. Walter Hooper (Grand Rapids, MI: Eerdmans, 1970), 66–67. The italics are Lewis's. Balder was the Norse god of light and joy, the son of the chief god, Odin. He was killed through the treachery of the trickster god, Loki, who made a dart of the one substance that he was vulnerable to, mistletoe, and gave it to another god who innocently threw it at him during a game. The whole world wept for Balder. Osiris was an Egyptian god of vegetation, who was killed and his body entombed in a tree. See Micha F. Lindemans, "Balder" and Katherine Fischer, "Osiris" in Encylopedia Mythica, http://www.pantheon.org/.

18. Ibid., 67.

19. Rachel Gross and Dale Grote, "Dionysus," in *Encylopedia Mythica,* http://www.pantheon.org/articles/d/dionysus.html.

20. Ruth Benedict, *Patterns of Culture* (New York: Houghton Mifflin, 1934).

21. *Prince Caspian*, 152.

22. Ibid., 154.

23. "Christian Apologetics," in *God in the Dock,* 101–2.

24. *Prince Caspian*, 154.

CHAPTER 8

1. See David Crumm, "Forty Strangers in a Virtual Room Talk about Religion," *Wired,* July 12, 2007.

2. *Surprised by Joy*, 59–60.

3. Ibid., 60.

4. Ibid.

5. Ibid., 60–61.

6. Ibid., 60.

7. *Prince Caspian*, 73.

8. Ibid., 163.

CHAPTER 9

1. I have written an entire book on this subject, *God at Work: Your Christian Vocation in All of Life* (Wheaton, IL: Crossway, 2002).

2. See my treatment of this passage in my book *State of the Arts: From Bezalel to Mapplethorpe* (Wheaton, IL: Crossway, 1991).

3. Christ, however, said that whoever does—or does not—feed the hungry, give a drink to the thirsty, welcome the stranger, clothe the naked, tend to the sick, and visit the prisoner does it (or does not do it) for Him (see Matt. 25:31–46). Just as God is hidden in our vocations, Christ is hidden in our neighbor. So we do serve God in our vocations after all. But the way He commands us to serve Him is to serve other people.

4. Einar Billing, *Our Calling* (Philadelphia: Fortress, 1964), 30.

5. See "The Table of Duties" in Luther's *Small Catechism,* in *Concordia: The Lutheran Confessions* (St. Louis: Concordia Publishing House, 2005), 372–4.

6. Max Weber, *The Protestant Ethic and the Spirit of Capitalism* (Oxford: Blackwell Publishers, 2002).

7. C. S. Lewis, "Learning in War-Time," in *The Weight of Glory and Other Addresses* (New York: HarperCollins, 2001), 55.

8. Ibid., 59.

9. Ibid.

10. Ibid., 58.

11. C. S. Lewis, *Perelandra* (New York: Scribner, 1996), 142.

12. Ibid., 142.

13. *Prince Caspian*, 200.

CHAPTER 10

1. *Prince Caspian*, 198.

2. M. Stanton Evans, *The Theme Is Freedom: Religion, Politics, and the American Tradition* (Washington, D.C.: Regnery, 1996).

3. The French Revolution is not in this tradition, since it was a secularized attempt at liberation through human reason alone. And because the human will is in bondage to sin, the French revolutionaries' distorted view of liberty evolved into the Reign of Terror and the dictatorship of Napoleon. The communist revolutions of Russia, China, Cambodia, and other countries were also of this kind—they also turned the people they purported to liberate into slaves.

4. *Prince Caspian*, 152.

5. See A. W. Pickard-Cambridge, *The Theatre of Dionysus in Athens* (Oxford: The Clarendon Press, 1946).

6. *Prince Caspian*, 191.

7. Ibid., 193.

8. Ibid., 194.

9. See my discussion of Lewis's attitude toward modern schools in my book *The Soul of the Lion, the Witch and the Wardrobe* (Colorado Springs: Victor Books, David C. Cook, 2005).

10. For a full account of both Lewis's own education and his views on education, see Joel D. Heck, *Irrigating Deserts: C. S. Lewis on Education* (St. Louis: Concordia Publishing House, 2006).

11. See Rudolf Flesch, *Why Johnny Can't Read: And What You Can Do About It* (New York: Harper and Brothers, 1955) and *Why Johnny Still Can't Read* (New

York: Harper Collins, 1983). In this latter book especially, Flesch thoroughly documents and dissects the modernist educational theory that lies behind many reading textbooks and shows how they kill the love of reading and the very ability to read well.

12. J. R. R. Tolkien, "On Fairy Stories," in *The Monsters and the Critics and Other Essays,* ed. Christopher Tolkien (Boston: Houghton Mifflin, 1984), 148.

13. *Prince Caspian,* 196.

14. Compare the attack of Tolkien's Ents on Saruman's forces in *The Two Towers.* Lewis's book was published in 1951, three years earlier than Tolkien's *The Lord of the Rings.* Lewis, though, had heard Tolkien read his book (in manuscript form) in gatherings of the Inklings.

CONCLUSION

1. *Prince Caspian,* 74.

2. Ibid., 74.

3. Ibid., 199.

4. As quoted in Baehr, 17.

5. "And you notice that I am guilty of a slight archaism in calling them 'rulers.' 'Leaders' is the modem word. I have suggested elsewhere that this is a deeply significant change of vocabulary. Our demand upon them has changed no less than theirs on us. For of a ruler one asks justice, incorruption, diligence, perhaps clemency; of a leader, dash, initiative, and (I suppose) what people call 'magnetism' or 'personality'" (*"De Descriptione Temporum"*).

6. "Christian Apologetics," in *God in the Dock,* 93.

7. C. S. Lewis, *The Great Divorce* (New York: HarperCollins, 2001), 118.